FROM THERE TO HERE

FROM THERE

CIARAN

CARSON

TO HERE

SELECTED POEMS AND TRANSLATIONS

First North American edition

Copyright © 2019 by Ciaran Carson

All rights reserved. No part of this book

may be reproduced in any form without prior

permission in writing from the publishers.

For permission, write to

Wake Forest University Press

Post Office Box 7333

Winston-Salem, NC 27109

wfupress.wfu.edu

wfupress@wfu.edu

ISBN 978-1-930630-88-8 (paperback)

LCCN 2018965403

Designed and typeset by Crisis

From There to Here was first published

by The Gallery Press in Ireland in 2018

and edited by Peter Fallon.

Publication of this book was generously

supported by the Boyle Family Fund.

Aistrigh liom siar sa ród

Journey back with me along the road

FROM THERE TO HERE

COLM CILLE RECITED

My hand is tired with writing out,
  my admirable nib not thick—
slender-beaked, my pen jets forth
a stream of beetle-coloured ink.

Deep the draught of wisdom coursing
  from my calligraphic hand
upon the page a screed of ink
made from the green-skinned holly leaf.

Unceasingly my little pen
transcribes a host of handsome books—
  enriching those who like to read,
and tiring out this hand that writes.

from the Middle Irish, *Colm Cille cecenit*

THE INSULAR CELTS

Having left solid ground behind
In the hardness of their placenames
They have sailed out for an island:

As along the top of a wood
Their boats have crossed the green ridges,
So has the pale sky overhead

Appeared as a milky surface,
A white plain where the speckled fish
Drift in lamb-white clouds of fleece.

They will come back to the warm earth
And call it by possessive names—
Thorned rose, love, woman and mother;

To hard hills of stone they will give
The words for breast; to meadowland,
The soft gutturals of rivers,

Tongues of water; to firm plains, flesh,
As one day we will discover
Their way of living in their death.

They entered their cold beds of soil
Not as graves, for this was the land
That they had fought for, loved, and killed

Each other for. They'd arrive again:
Death could be no horizon
But the shoreline of their island,

A coming and going, as flood
Comes after ebb. In the spirals
Of their brooches is seen the flight

Of one thing into the other:
As the wheel-ruts on a battle-
Plain have filled with silver water,

The confused circles of their wars,
Their cattle-raids, have worked themselves
To a laced pattern of old scars.

But their death, since it is no real
Death, will happen over again
And again, their bones will seem still

To fall in the hail beneath hooves
Of horses, their limbs will drift down
As the branches that trees have loosed.

We cannot yet say why or how
They could not take things as they were.
Someday we will learn of how

Their bronze swords took the shape of leaves,
How their gold spears are found in cornfields,
Their arrows are found in trees.

THE BOMB DISPOSAL

Is it just like picking a lock
With the slow deliberation of a funeral,
Hesitating through a darkened nave
Until you find the answer?

Listening to the malevolent tick
Of its heart, can you read
The message of the threaded veins
Like print, its body's chart?

The city is a map of the city,
Its forbidden areas changing daily.
I find myself in a crowded taxi
Making deviations from the known route,

Ending in a cul-de-sac
Where everyone breaks out suddenly
In whispers, noting the boarded windows,
The drawn blinds.

TWINE

My father's postman sack
Hung on a nail behind the kitchen door,
Its yellow straps undone. I stuck my head inside
The canvas flap and breathed the gloom.

The smell of raffia and faded ink
Was like the smell of nothing. The twine lay in
My mother's bottom drawer, the undelivered
Letters were returned to sender.

I thought of being shut up under stairs.
Outside it was snowing, and my father's hands
Were blue with cold. Soon he would return,
His hands would warm me.

Christmas came. He worked all day.
His dinner would be kept hot in the oven.
There was the twine to tie the turkey's legs.
There was the tawse behind the kitchen door.

RUBBISH

From the sick-room window, past
The leaning-sideways
Railway sleepers of the fence,
The swaying nettles,
You can just make out
The rusty fire of a crushed
Coke tin, the dotted glint of staples in
A wet cardboard box.

I could be sifting through
The tip at the bottom of Ganges Street.
Eggshells. Bricks. A broken hypodermic,
And one bit of plaster
Painted on one side
I seem to recognize from somewhere—

It is the off-white wall
I stared at as a child
As my mother picked my hair for nits.
The iron comb scraped out
A series of indefinite ticks
As they dropped on a double leaf
Of last week's *Irish News*.
I had a crick in my neck.

I thought that someone
On the last train might look up
And see me staring out beyond
The almost-useless strip
Between the railway
And the new industrial estate.

CÉILÍ

If there was a house with three girls in it
It only took three boys to make a dance.
You'd see a glimmer where McKeown's once was
And follow it till it became a house.
But maybe they'd have gone on, up the hill
To Loughran's, or made across the grazing,
Somewhere else. All those twistings and turnings,
Crossroads and dirt roads and skittery lanes:
You'd be glad to get in from the dark.

And when you did get in there'd be a power
Of *poitín*. A big tin creamery churn,
A ladle, those mugs with blue and white bars.
Oh, good and clear like the best of water.
The music would start up. This one ould boy
Would sit by the fire and rosin away,
Sawing and sawing till it fell like snow.
That *poitín* was quare stuff. At the end of
The night you might be fiddling with no bow.

When everyone was ready out would come
The tin of Tate and Lyle's Golden Syrup,
A spoon or a knife, a big farl of bread.
Some of those same boys wouldn't bother with
The way you were supposed to screw it up.
There might be courting going on outside,
Whisperings and cacklings in the barnyard;
A spider thread of gold-thin syrup
Trailed out across the glowing kitchen tiles
Into the night of promises, or broken promises.

SOOT

It was autumn. First, she shrouded
The furniture, then rolled back the carpet
As if for dancing; then moved
The ornaments from the mantelpiece,
Afraid his roughness might disturb
Their staid fragility.

He came; shyly, she let him in,
Feeling ill-at-ease in the newly-spacious
Room, her footsteps sounding hollow
On the boards. She watched him kneel
Before the hearth, and said something
About the weather. He did not answer,

Too busy with his work for speech.
The stem of yellow cane creaked upwards
Tentatively. After a while he asked
Her to go outside and look, and there,
Above the roof, she saw the frayed sunflower
Bloom triumphantly. She came back

And asked how much she owed him, grimacing
As she put the money in his soiled hand.
When he had gone a weightless hush
Lingered in the house for days. Slowly,
It settled; the fire burned cleanly;
Everything was spotless.

Hearing that soot was good for the soil
She threw it on the flowerbeds. She would watch
It crumble, dissolving in the rain,
Finding its way to lightless crevices,
Sleeping, till in spring it would emerge softly
As the ink-bruise in the pansy's heart.

DUNNE

It was then I heard of the missing man.
The wireless spoke through a hiss of static—
Someone was being interviewed:
*The missing man, the caller said, can be found
At Cullyhanna Parochial House.*
That was all. Those were his very words.
I reached an avenue of darkened yews.
Somewhere footsteps on the gravel.

*I then identified myself, and he
Embraced me, someone I had never seen
Before, but it was him all right, bearded
And dishevelled. There were tears in his eyes.
He knew nothing of the ransoms.
He did not know who they were. He knew nothing
Of his whereabouts. He did not even know
If he was in the South or North.*

It seemed he was relieved from hiding in
Some outhouse filled with ploughs and harrows,
Rusted winnowings that jabbed and rasped
At him. He had felt like a beaten child.
When they hooded him with a balaklava
He thought the woolly blackness was like being
Shut up under stairs, without a hint of hope,
Stitches dropped that no one could knit back.

From Camlough, Silverbridge and Crossmaglen
The military were closing in. He was,
It seemed, the paste on the wallpaper, or

The wall, spunked out between the leaves, etched
At last into the memories of what might have been.
He was released. The three bullets they had given him
As souvenirs chinked in his pocket. He slipped
Through a hole in the security net.

All day long for seven days he had lain
On the broad of his back on the floor.
He could see nothing, but turned, again
And again, to an image of himself as a child
Hunched in bed, staring at the ceiling,
At the enigmatic pits and tics
That scored the blankness, and then, farther,
To the stars that brushed against the windowpane.

SMITHFIELD

I have forgotten something, I am
Going back. The wrought-iron flowers
Of the gate breathe open to
Sooty alcoves, the withered shelves
Of books. There is a light
That glints off tin and earthenware
Reminding me of touch, the beaded moulding
Of a picture frame—

Here is a hand that beckons from
An empty doorway. Open the gilt clasp,
The book of strangers:
The families arranged with roses,
The brothers, the sister
In her First Communion frock, their hands
Like ornaments in mine beneath
The muffled ribs of gloves.

We are all walking to school
Past the face of a clock, linked
Together in the glass dark of the
Undertaker's window: one, two, three, four
Figures in the gilt lettering.
Soon it will be dusk, and all of us are sent
To find each other, though each
Of us is lost in a separate field:

Over the waving meadow, through
The trees, a gap of light sways
Like a face, a hand discovering itself

Among the branches and the inlets.
One of us has fallen in the river,
The stream of my mother's veil at the porch,
Sunlight on a brick wall smiling
With the child who is not there.

PATCHWORK

It was only just this minute that I noticed the perfectly triangular
Barbed wire rip in the sleeve of my shirt, and wondered where I'd got it.
I'd crossed no fences that I knew about. Then it struck me: an almost identical
Tear in my new white Sunday shirt, when I was six. My mother, after her initial
Nagging, stitched it up. But you can never make a perfect job on tears like that.
Eventually she cut it up for handkerchiefs: six neatly-hemmed squares.
Snags of greyish wool remind me of the mountain that we climbed that day—
Nearly at the summit, we could see the map of Belfast. My father stopped
For a cigarette and pointed out the landmarks: Gallaher's tobacco factory,
Clonard Monastery, the invisible speck of our house, lost in all the rows
And terraces and furrows, like this one sheep that's strayed into the rags
And bandages that flock the holy well. A little stack of ball-point pens,
Some broken spectacles, a walking stick, two hearing-aids: prayers
Repeated and repeated until granted.

                              So when I saw, last week, the crucifix
Earring dangling from the right ear of this young Charismatic
Christian fiddle-player, I could not help but think of beads, beads
Told over and over—like my father's rosary of olive stones from
Mount Olive, I think, that he had thumbed and fingered so much the decades
Missed a pip or two. The cross itself was ebony and silver, just like
This young girl's, that swung and tinkled like a thurible. She was playing
'The Teetotaller'. Someone had to buy a drink just then, of course: a pint of Harp,
Four pints of stout, two Paddy whiskies, and a bottle of Lucozade—the baby
Version, not the ones you get in hospital, wrapped in crackling see-through
Cellophane. You remember how you held it to the light, and light shone
    through?
The opposite of Polaroids, really, the world filmed in dazzling sunshine:
A quite unremarkable day of mist and drizzle. The rainy hush of traffic,
Muted car horns, a dog making a dog-leg walk across a zebra crossing . . .
As the lights changed from red to green and back to red again
I fingered the eighteen stitches in the puckered mouth of my appendicectomy.

The doctor's waiting room, now that I remember it, had a print of *The Angelus*
Above the fireplace; sometimes, waiting for the buzzer, I'd hear the Angelus
Itself boom out from St Peter's. With only two or three deliberate steps
I could escape into the frame, unnoticed by the peasant and his wife. I'd vanish
Into sepia. The last shivering bell would die on the wind.
I was in the surgery. Stainless steel and hypodermics glinted on the shelves.
Now I saw my mother: the needle shone between her thumb and finger,
          stitching,
Darning, mending: the woolly callous on a sock, the unravelled jumper
That became a scarf. I held my arms at arms' length as she wound and wound:
The tick-tack of the knitting needles made a cable-knit pullover.
Come Christmas morning I would wear it, with a new white shirt unpinned
From its cardboard stiffener.
                              I shivered at the touch of cold white linen—
A mild shock, as if, when almost sleeping, you'd dreamt you'd fallen
Suddenly, and realized now you were awake: the curtains fluttered
In the breeze across the open window, exactly as they had before. Everything
Was back to normal. Outside, the noise of children playing: a tin can kicked
Across a tarred road, the whip-whop of a skipping rope, singing—
Poor Toby is dead and he lies in his grave, lies in his grave, lies in his grave . . .
So, the nicotine-stained bone buttons on my father's melodeon clicked
And ticked as he wheezed his way through *Oft in the Stilly Night*—or,
For that matter, *Nearer My God to Thee*, which he'd play on Sundays, just before
He went to see my granny, after Mass. Sometimes she'd be sick—*Another
Clean shirt'll do me*—and we'd climb the narrow stair to where she lay, buried
Beneath the patchwork quilt.
                              It took me twenty years to make that quilt—
I'm speaking for her now—and, *Your father's stitched into that quilt,
Your uncles and your aunts.* She'd take a sip from the baby Power's
On the bedside table. *Anything that came to hand, a bit of cotton print,
A poplin tie: I snipped them all up.* I could see her working in the gloom,
The shadow of the quilt draped round her knees. A needle shone between
Her thumb and finger. Minutes, hours of stitches threaded patiently; my father

Tugged at her, a stitch went wrong; she started up again. *You drink your tea*
Just like your father: two sups and a gulp: and so I'd see a mirror image
Raise the cup and take two sips, and swallow, or place my cup exactly on
The brown ring stain on the white damask tablecloth.

Davy's gone to England,
Rosie to America; who'll be next, I don't know. Yet they all came back.
I'd hardly know them now. The last time I saw them all together was
The funeral. As the Rosary was said I noticed how my father handled the invisible
Bead on the last decade: a gesture he'd repeat again at the graveside.
A shower of hail: far away, up on the mountain, a cloud of sheep had scattered
In the Hatchet Field. *The stitches show in everything I've made*, she'd say—
The quilt was meant for someone's wedding, but it never got that far.
And some one of us has it now, though who exactly I don't know.

CAMPAIGN

They had questioned him for hours. Who exactly was he? And when
He told them, they questioned him again. When they accepted who he was, as
Someone not involved, they pulled out his fingernails. Then
They took him to a waste-ground somewhere near The Horseshoe Bend, and
    told him
What he was. They shot him nine times.

A dark umbilicus of smoke was rising from a heap of burning tyres.
The bad smell he smelt was the smell of himself. Broken glass and knotted
    Durex.
The knuckles of a face in a nylon stocking. I used to see him in The Gladstone
    Bar,
Drawing pints for strangers, his almost-perfect fingers flecked with scum.

COCKTAILS

Bombing at about ninety miles an hour with the exhaust skittering
The skid-marked pitted tarmac of Kennedy Way, they hit the ramp and sailed
Clean over the red-and-white guillotine of the checkpoint and landed
On the M1 flyover, then disappeared before the Brits knew what hit them. So
The story went: we were in the Whip & Saddle bar of the Europa.

There was talk of someone who was shot nine times and lived, and someone
    else
Had the inside info on the Romper Room. We were trying to remember the
    facts
Behind the Black & Decker case, when someone ordered another drink and
    we entered
The realm of Jabberwocks and Angels' Wings, Widows' Kisses, Corpse
    Revivers.

THE IRISH FOR NO

Was it a vision, or a waking dream? I heard her voice before I saw
What looked like the balcony scene in *Romeo and Juliet*, except Romeo
Seemed to have shinned up a pipe and was inside arguing with her. The
    casements
Were wide open and I could see some Japanese-style wall-hangings, the
    dangling
Quotation marks of a yin-yang mobile. *It's got nothing*, she was snarling,
    nothing
To do with politics, and, before the bamboo curtain came down, *That goes for*
    you too!

It was time to turn into the dog-leg short cut from Chlorine Gardens
Into Cloreen Park, where you might see an *Ulster Says No* scrawled on the side
Of the power-block—which immediately reminds me of The Eglantine Inn
Just on the corner: on the missing *h* of Cloreen, you might say. We were
    debating,
Bacchus and the pards and me, how to render *The Ulster Bank—the Bank*
That Likes to Say Yes into Irish, and whether eglantine was alien to Ireland.
I cannot see what flowers are at my feet, when *yes* is the verb repeated,
Not exactly yes, but phatic nods and whispers. *The Bank That Answers All*
Your Questions, maybe? That Greek portico of Mourne granite, dazzling
With promises and feldspar, mirrors you in the Delphic black of its
    windows.

And the bruised pansies of the funeral parlour are dying in reversed gold
    letters,
The long sigh of the afternoon is not yet complete on the promontory where
    the victim,
A corporal in the UDR from Lisbellaw, was last seen having driven over half
Of Ulster, a legally-held gun was found and the incidence of stress came up

On the headland which shadows Larne Harbour and the black pitch of
    warehouses.
There is a melancholy blast of diesel, a puff of smoke which might be black
    or white.
So the harbour slips away to perilous seas as things remain unsolved; we
    listen
To the *ex cathedra* of the foghorn, and *drink and leave the world unseen*—

What's all this to the Belfast businessman who drilled
Thirteen holes in his head with a Black & Decker? It was just a normal
    morning
When they came. The tennis court shone with dew or frost, a little before
    dawn.
The border, it seemed, was not yet crossed: the Milky Way trailed snowy
    brambles,
The stars clustered thick as blackberries. They opened the door into the dark:
The murmurous haunt of flies on summer eves. Empty jam-jars.
Mish-mash. Hotch-potch. And now you rub your eyes and get acquainted
    with the light
A dust of something reminiscent drowses over the garage smell of creosote,
The concrete: blue clouds in porcelain, a paintbrush steeped in a chipped
    cup;
Staples hyphenate a wet cardboard box as the upturned can of oil still spills
And the unfed cat toys with the yin-yang of a tennis ball, debating whether
    yes is *no.*

ARMY

The duck patrol is waddling down the odd-numbers side of Raglan Street,
The bass-ackwards private at the rear trying not to think of a third eye
Being drilled in the back of his head. 55. They stop. The head
Peers round, then leaps the gap of Balaklava Street. He waves the body over
One by one. 49. Cape Street. A gable wall. Garnet Street. A gable wall.

Frere Street. 47. 45½. Milan Street. A grocer's shop.
They stop. They check their guns. 13. Milton Street. An iron lamp post.
No. 1. Ormond Street. *Two ducks in front of a duck and two ducks
Behind a duck, how many ducks? Five? No. Three. This is not the end.*

BELFAST CONFETTI

Suddenly as the riot squad moved in it was raining exclamation marks,
Nuts, bolts, nails, car-keys. A fount of broken type. And the explosion
Itself—an asterisk on the map. This hyphenated line, a burst of rapid fire . . .
I was trying to complete a sentence in my head, but it kept stuttering,
All the alleyways and side streets blocked with stops and colons.

I know this labyrinth so well—Balaklava, Raglan, Inkerman, Odessa Street—
Why can't I escape? Every move is punctuated. Crimea Street. Dead end
    again.
A Saracen, Kremlin-2 mesh. Makrolon face-shields. Walkie-talkies. What is
My name? Where am I coming from? Where am I going? A fusillade of
    question marks.

DRESDEN

Horse Boyle was called Horse Boyle because of his brother Mule;
Though why Mule was called Mule is anybody's guess. I stayed there once,
Or rather, I nearly stayed there once. But that's another story.
At any rate they lived in this decrepit caravan, not two miles out of Carrick,
Encroached upon by baroque pyramids of empty baked bean tins, rusts
And ochres, hints of autumn merging into twilight. Horse believed
They were as good as a watchdog, and to tell you the truth
You couldn't go near the place without something falling over:
A minor avalanche would ensue—more like a shop bell, really,

The old-fashioned ones on string, connected to the latch, I think,
And as you entered in, the bell would tinkle in the empty shop, a musk
Of soap and turf and sweets would hit you from the gloom. Tobacco.
Baling wire. Twine. And, of course, shelves and pyramids of tins.
An old woman would appear from the back—there was a sizzling pan in
     there
Somewhere, a whiff of eggs and bacon—and ask you what you wanted;
Or rather, she wouldn't ask; she would talk about the weather. It had rained
That day, but it was looking better. They had just put in the spuds.
I had only come to pass the time of day, so I bought a token packet of Gold
     Leaf.

All this time the fry was frying away. Maybe she'd a daughter in there
Somewhere, though I hadn't heard the neighbours talk of it; if anybody
     knew,
It would be Horse. Horse kept his ears to the ground.
And he was a great man for current affairs; he owned the only TV in the
     place.
Come dusk he'd set off on his rounds, to tell the whole town-land the latest
Situation in the Middle East, a mortar bomb attack in Mullaghbawn—

The damn things never worked, of course—and so he'd tell the story
How in his young day it was very different. Take young Flynn, for instance,
Who was ordered to take this bus and smuggle some sticks of gelignite

Across the border, into Derry, when the RUC—or was it the RIC?—
Got wind of it. The bus was stopped, the peeler stepped on. Young Flynn
Took it like a man, of course: he owned up right away. He opened the bag
And produced the bomb, his rank and serial number. For all the world
Like a pound of sausages. Of course, the thing was, the peeler's bike
Had got a puncture, and he didn't know young Flynn from Adam. All he
    wanted
Was to get home for his tea. Flynn was in for seven years and learned to
    speak
The best of Irish. He had thirteen words for a cow in heat;
A word for the third thwart in a boat; the wake of a boat on the ebb tide.
He knew the extinct names of insects, flowers, why this place was called
Whatever: *Carrick*, for example, was a *rock*. He was damn right there—
As the man said, *When you buy meat you buy bones, when you buy land you
    buy stones.*
You'd be hard put to find a square foot in the whole bloody parish
That wasn't thick with flints and pebbles. To this day he could hear the grate
And scrape as the spade struck home, for it reminded him of broken bones:
Digging a graveyard, maybe—or better still, trying to dig a reclaimed tip
Of broken delft and crockery ware—you know that sound that sets your
    teeth on edge
When the chalk squeaks on the blackboard, or you shovel ashes from the
    stove?

Master McGinty—he'd be on about McGinty then, and discipline, the
    capitals
Of South America, Moore's *Melodies*, the Battle of Clontarf, and
Tell me this, an educated man like you: What goes on four legs when it's young,

Two legs when it's grown up, and three legs when it's old? I'd pretend
I didn't know. McGinty's leather strap would come up then, stuffed
With threepenny bits to give it weight and sting. Of course it never did him
Any harm: *You could take a horse to water but you couldn't make him drink.*
He himself was nearly going on to be a priest.
And many's the young cub left the school as wise as when he came.
Carrowkeel was where McGinty came from—*Narrow Quarter*, Flynn
    explained—
Back before the Troubles, a place that was so mean and crabbed,
Horse would have it, men were known to eat their dinner from a drawer.
Which they'd slide shut the minute you'd walk in.
He'd demonstrate this at the kitchen table, hunched and furtive, squinting
Out the window—past the teetering minarets of rust, down the hedge-dark
    aisle—
To where a stranger might appear, a passerby, or what was maybe worse,
Someone he knew. Someone who wanted something. Someone who was
    hungry.
Of course who should come tottering up the lane that instant but his brother

Mule. I forgot to mention they were twins. They were as like two—
No, not peas in a pod, for this is not the time nor the place to go into
Comparisons, and this is really Horse's story, Horse who—now I'm getting
Round to it—flew over Dresden in the war. He'd emigrated first, to
Manchester. Something to do with scrap—redundant mill machinery,
Giant flywheels, broken looms that would, eventually, be ships, or
    aeroplanes.
He said he wore his fingers to the bone.
And so, on impulse, he had joined the RAF. He became a rear gunner.
Of all the missions, Dresden broke his heart. It reminded him of china.
As he remembered it, long afterwards, he could hear, or almost hear,
Between the rapid desultory thunderclaps, a thousand tinkling echoes—
All across the map of Dresden, storerooms full of china shivered, teetered

And collapsed, an avalanche of porcelain, slushing and cascading: cherubs,
Shepherdesses, figurines of Hope and Peace and Victory, delicate bone
    fragments.
He recalled in particular a figure from his childhood, a milkmaid
Standing on the mantelpiece. Each night as they knelt down for the Rosary
His eyes would wander up to where she seemed to beckon to him, smiling,
Offering him, eternally, her pitcher of milk, her mouth of rose and cream.

One day, reaching up to hold her yet again, his fingers stumbled, and she fell.
He lifted down a biscuit tin, and opened it.
It breathed an antique incense: things like pencils, snuff, tobacco.
His war medals. A broken rosary. And there, the milkmaid's creamy hand, the
    outstretched
Pitcher of milk, all that survived. Outside, there was a scraping
And a tittering; I knew Mule's step by now, his careful drunken weaving
Through the tin-stacks. I might have stayed the night, but there's no time
To go back to that now; I could hardly, at any rate, pick up the thread.
I wandered out through the steeples of rust, the gate that was a broken bed.

CLEARANCE

The Royal Avenue Hotel collapses under the breaker's pendulum:
Zigzag stairwells, chimney-flues, and a Thirties mural
Of an elegantly-dressed couple doing what seems to be the Tango, in
    Wedgewood
Blue and white—happy days! Suddenly more sky
Than there used to be. A breeze springs up from nowhere—

There, through a gap in the rubble, a greengrocer's shop
I'd never noticed until now. Or had I passed it yesterday? Everything—
Yellow, green and purple—is fresh as paint. Rain glistens on the aubergines
And peppers; even from this distance the potatoes smell of earth.

TURN AGAIN

There is a map of the city which shows the bridge that was never built.
A map which shows the bridge that collapsed; the streets that never
    existed.
Ireland's Entry, Elbow Lane, Weigh-House Lane, Back Lane, Stone-Cutter's
    Entry—
Today's plan is already yesterday's—the streets that were there are gone.
And the shape of the jails cannot be shown for security reasons.

The linen backing is falling apart—the Falls Road hangs by a thread.
When someone asks me where I live, I remember where I used to live.
Someone asks me for directions, and I think again. I turn into
A side street to try to throw off my shadow, and history is changed.

SNOW

A white dot flicked back and forth across the bay window: not
A table-tennis ball, but 'ping-pong', since this is happening in another era,
The extended leaves of the dining table—scratched mahogany veneer—
Suggesting many such encounters, or time passing: the celluloid diminuendo
As it bounces off into a corner and ticks to an incorrigible stop.
I pick it up days later, trying to get that pallor right: it's neither ivory
Nor milk. Chalk is better; and there's a hint of pearl, translucent
Lurking just behind opaque. I broke open the husk so many times
And always found it empty; the pith was a wordless bubble.

Though there's nothing in the thing itself, bits of it come back unbidden,
Playing in the archaic dusk till the white blip became invisible.
Just as, the other day, I felt the tacky pimples of a ping-pong bat
When the bank clerk counted out my money with her rubber thimble, and
    knew
The black was bleeding into red. Her face was snow and roses just behind
The bulletproof glass: I couldn't touch her if I tried. I crumpled up the chit—
No use in keeping what you haven't got—and took a stroll to Ross's auction.
There was this Thirties scuffed leather sofa I wanted to make a bid for.
Gestures, prices: soundlessly collateral in the murmuring room.

I won't say what I paid for it: anything's too much when you have nothing.
But in the dark recesses underneath the cushions I found myself kneeling
As decades of the Rosary dragged by, the slack of years ago hauled up
Bead by bead; and with them, all the haberdashery of loss—cuff buttons,
Broken ballpoint pens and fluff, old pennies, pins and needles, and yes,
A ping-pong ball. I cupped it in my hands like a crystal, seeing not
The future, but a shadowed parlour just before the blinds are drawn. Someone
Has put up two trestles. Handshakes all round, nods and whispers.
Roses are brought in and, suddenly, white confetti seethes against the window.

LAST ORDERS

Squeeze the buzzer on the steel mesh gate like a trigger, but
It's someone else who has you in their sights. *Click*. It opens. Like electronic
Russian roulette, since you never know for sure who's who, or what
You're walking into. I, for instance, could be anybody. Though I'm told
Taig's written on my face. See me, would *I* trust appearances?

Inside a sudden lull. The barman lolls his head at us. We order Harp—
Seems safe enough, everybody drinks it. As someone looks daggers at us
From the Bushmills mirror, a penny drops: how simple it would be for
    someone
Like ourselves to walk in and blow the whole place, and ourselves, to
    Kingdom Come.

AMBITION

I did not allow myself to think of ultimate escape . . . one step at a time was enough.
—JOHN BUCHAN, *Mr Standfast*

Now I've climbed this far it's time to look back. But smoke obscures
The panorama from the Mountain Loney spring. The city and the mountain
   are on fire.
My mouth's still stinging from the cold sharp shock of water—a winter taste
In summer—but my father's wandered off somewhere. I can't seem to find
   him.
We'd been smoking 'coffin nails', and he'd been talking of his time inside,
   how
Matches were that scarce you'd have to split them four ways with your
   thumbnail;
And seven cigarette ends made a cigarette. *Keep a thing for seven years,*
You'll always find a use for it, he follows in the same breath . . . it reminds me
Of the saint who, when he had his head cut off, picked up his head and
   walked
With it for seven miles. And the wise man said, *The distance doesn't matter,*
It's the first step that was difficult.

Any journey's like that—*the first step of your life,* my father interrupts—
Though often you take one step forward, two steps back. For if time is a road
It's fraught with ramps and dog-legs, switchbacks and spaghetti; here and
   there,
The dual carriageway becomes a one-track, backward mind. And bits of the
   landscape
Keep recurring: it seems as if I've watched the same suburban tennis match
For hours, and heard, at ever less-surprising intervals, the applause of
   pigeons
Bursting from a loft. Or the issue is not yet decided, as the desultory
   handclaps

Turn to rain. The window that my nose is pressed against is breathed-on,
    giving
Everything a sfumato air. I keep drawing faces on it, or practising my
    signature.

And if time is a road, then you're checked again and again
By a mobile checkpoint. One soldier holds a gun to your head. Another
    soldier
Asks you questions, and another checks the information on the head
    computer.
Your name. Your brothers' names. Your father's name. His occupation. As if
The one they're looking for is not you, but it might be you. Looks like you
Or smells like you. And suddenly, the posthumous aroma of an empty
    canvas
Postman's sack—twine, ink, dead letters—wafts out from the soldiers'
Sodden khaki. It's obvious they're bored: one of them is watching
    Wimbledon
On one of those postage-stamp-sized TV screens. *Of course, the proper shot,*
An unseen talking head intones, *should have been the lob.* He's using words
    like
Angled, volley, smash and *strategy.* Someone is *fighting a losing battle.*
Isn't that the way, that someone tells you what you should have done, when
You've just done the opposite? Did you give the orders for this man's death?
On the contrary, the accused replies, as if he'd ordered birth or resurrection.
Though *one nail drives out another,* as my father says.

And my father should have known better than to tamper with Her Majesty's
Royal Mail—or was it His, then? His humour was to take an Irish ha'penny
With the harp on the flip side, and frank a letter with it. Some people didn't
See the joke; they'd always thought him a Republican. He was reported,
Laid off for a month. Which is why he never got promoted. So one story
    goes.

The other is a war-time one, where he's supposed to go to England
For a training course, but doesn't, seeing he doesn't want to get conscripted.
My mother's version is he lacked ambition. He was too content to stay
In one place. He liked things as they were . . . *perfect touch, perfect timing,*
     perfect
Accuracy: the commentary has just nudged me back a little, as I manage
To take in the action replay. There's a tiny puff of chalk, as the ball skids off
The line, like someone might be firing in slow motion, far away: that
     otherwise
Unnoticeable faint cloud on the summer blue, which makes the sky around
     it
All the more intense and fragile.

It's nearer to a winter blue. A zigzag track of footsteps is imprinted
On the frosted tennis court: it looks as if the Disappeared One rose before
First light, and stalked from one side of the wire cage to the other, off
Into the glinting laurels. No armed wing has yet proclaimed responsibility:
One hand washes the other, says my father, *as sure as one funeral makes many.*
For the present is a tit-for-tat campaign, exchanging *now* for *then,*
The Christmas post of Christmas Past, the black armband of the temporary
     man;
The insignia have mourned already for this casual preserve. Threading
Through the early morning suburbs and the monkey-puzzle trees, a smell of
     coffee lingers,
Imprisoned in the air like wisps of orange peel in marmalade; and sleigh-bell
     music
Tinkles on the radio, like ice cubes in a summer drink. I think I'm starting,
     now,
To know the street map with my feet, just like my father.

God never shuts one door, said my father, *but he opens up another*; and then,
I walked the iron catwalk naked in the freezing cold: he's back into his time

As internee, the humiliation of the weekly bath. It was seven weeks before
He was released: it was his younger brother they were after all the time.
God never opens one door, but he shuts another: my uncle was inside for seven
  years.
At his funeral they said how much I looked like him: I've got his smoker's
  cough,
At any rate. And now my father's told to cut down on the cigarettes he
  smokes
Them three or four puffs at a time. Stubs them out and lights them, seven
  times.
I found him yesterday a hundred yards ahead of me, struggling, as the
  blazing
Summer hauled him one step at a time into a freezing furnace. And with
  each step
He aged. As I closed in on him, he coughed. I coughed. He stopped and
  turned,
Made two steps back towards me, and I took one step forward.

YES

I'm drinking in the 7-Up bottle-green eyes of the barmaid
On the *Enterprise* express—bottles and glasses clinking each other—
When the train slows with a noise like *Schweppes* and halts just outside
   Dundalk.
Not that unwontedly, since we're no strangers to the border bomb.
As the Belfast accent of the tannoy tells us what is happening

I'm about to quote from Bashō's *The Narrow Road to the Deep North*—
Blossoming mushroom: from some unknown tree a leaf has stuck to it—
When it goes off and we're thrown out of kilter. My mouth is full
Of broken glass and quinine as everything reverses South.

BLOODY HAND

Your man, says the Man, *will walk into the bar like this*—here his fingers
Mimic a pair of legs, one stiff at the knee—*so you'll know exactly*
What to do. He sticks a finger to his head. Pretend it's child's play—
The hand might be a horse's mouth, a rabbit or a dog. Five handclaps.
Walls have ears: the shadows you throw are the shadows you try to throw off.

I snuffed out the candle between finger and thumb. Was it the left hand
Hacked off at the wrist and thrown to the shores of Ulster? Did Ulster
Exist? Or the Right Hand of God, saying *Stop* to this and *No* to that?
My thumb is the hammer of a gun. The thumb goes up. The thumb goes
    down.

HAMLET

As usual, the clock in The Clock Bar was a good few minutes fast:
A fiction no one really bothered to maintain, unlike the story
The comrade on my left was telling, which no one knew for certain truth:
Back in 1922, a sergeant, I forget his name, was shot outside the National Bank . . .
Ah yes, what year was it that they knocked it down? Yet, its memory's as fresh
As the inky smell of new pound notes—which interferes with the beer-and-
 whiskey
Tang of now, like two dogs meeting in the revolutionary 69 of a long sniff,
Or cattle jostling shit-stained flanks in the Pound. For *pound*, as some wag
Interrupted, was an offshoot of the Falls, from the Irish, *fál*, a hedge;
Hence, *any kind of enclosed thing*, its twigs and branches commemorated
By the soldiers' drab and olive camouflage, as they try to melt
Into a brick wall; red coats might be better, after all. *At any rate*,
This sergeant's number came up; not a winning one. The bullet had his name on it.
Though Sergeant X, as we'll call him, doesn't really feature in the story:
The nub of it is, *This tin can which was heard that night, trundling down*
From the bank, down Balaklava Street. Which thousands heard, and no one ever
Saw. Which was heard for years, any night that trouble might be
Round the corner . . . and when it skittered to a halt, you knew
That someone else had snuffed it: a name drifting like an afterthought,
A scribbled wisp of smoke you try and grasp, as it becomes diminuendo, then
Vanishes. For *fál* is also *frontier, boundary*, as in *the undiscovered country*
From whose bourne no traveller returns, the illegible, thorny hedge of time
 itself—
Heartstopping moments, measured not by the pulse of a wristwatch, nor
The archaic anarchists' alarm clock, but a mercury tilt device
Which 'only connects' on any given bump on the road. So, by this wingèd
 messenger
The promise 'to pay the bearer' is fulfilled:

As someone buys another round, an Allied Irish Banks £10 note drowns in
The slops of the counter; a Guinness stain blooms on the artist's impression
Of the sinking of the *Girona*; a tiny foam hisses round the salamander brooch
Dredged up to show how love and money endure, beyond death and the
    Armada,
Like the bomb-disposal expert in his suit of salamander cloth.
Shielded against the blast of time by a strangely mediaeval visor,
He's been outmoded by this jerky robot whose various attachments include
A large hook for turning over corpses that may be booby-trapped;
But I still have this picture of his hands held up to avert the future
In a final act of *No surrender*, as, twisting through the murky fathoms
Of what might have been, he is washed ashore as pearl and coral.

This *strange eruption to our state* is seen in other versions of the Falls:
A no-go area, a ghetto, a demolition zone. For the ghost, as it turns out—
All this according to your man, and I can well believe it—this tin ghost,
Since the streets it haunted were abolished, was never heard again.
The sleeve of Raglan Street has been unravelled; the helmet of Balaklava
Is torn away from the mouth. The dim glow of Garnet has gone out,
And with it, all but the memory of where I lived. I, too, heard the ghost:
A roulette trickle, or the hesitant annunciation of a downpour, ricocheting
Off the window; a goods train shunting distantly into a siding,
Then groaning to a halt; the rainy cries of children after dusk.
For the voice from the grave reverberates in others' mouths, as the sails
Of the whitethorn hedge swell up in a little breeze, and tremble
Like the spiral blossom of Andromeda: so suddenly are shrouds and branches
Hung with street lights, celebrating all that's lost, as fields are reclaimed
By the Starry Plough. So we name the constellations, to put a shape
On what was there; so, the storyteller picks his way between the isolated stars.

But, *Was it really like that?* And, *Is the story true?*
You might as well tear off the iron mask, and find that no one, after all,

Is there: nothing but a cry, a summons, clanking out from the smoke
Of demolition. Like some son looking for his father, or the father for his son,
We try to piece together the exploded fragments. Let these broken spars
Stand for the Armada and its proud full sails, for even if
The clock is put to rights, everyone will still believe it's fast:
The barman's shouts of *Time* will be ignored in any case, since time
Is conversation; it is the hedge that flits incessantly into the present,
As words blossom from the speakers' mouths, and the flotilla returns to
      harbour,
Long after hours.

NIGHT OUT

Every Thursday night when we press the brass button on the galvanized wire
    mesh gate
A figure appears momentarily at the end of the strip-lit concrete
    passageway,
Then disappears. The gate squeaks open, slams shut almost instantly behind
    us.
Then through the semi-opaque heavy-duty polythene swing doors they
    might have taken
From a hospital. At the bar we get the once-over once again.

Seven whiskeys later the band is launching into 'Four Green Fields'.
From somewhere out beyond the breeze-block walls we get a broken rhythm
Of machine-gun fire. A ragged chorus. So the sentence of the night
Is punctuated through and through by rounds of drink, of bullets, of
    applause.

SWITCH

from the Irish of Seán Ó Ríordáin, 'Malairt'

'Come over here,' said Turnbull, 'till you see the sorrow
     in the horse's eyes.
Had you such heavy hooves as these for feet, there would
     be sorrow in your eyes too.'

And it was clear to me, that he'd realized the sorrow
     in the horse's eyes so well,
had dwelled so much on it, that he was steeped
     in the horse's mind.

I looked at the horse, that I might see the sorrow
     standing its eyes,
and saw the eyes of Turnbull looking at me
     from the horse's head.

I looked at Turnbull; I looked twice at him,
     and saw in that face of his
the over-big eyes that were dumb with sorrow—
     the horse's eyes.

SECOND LANGUAGE

English not being yet a language, I wrapped my lubber-lips around my
    thumb;
Brain-deaf as an embryo, I was snuggled in my comfort-blanket dumb.

Growling figures campaniled above me, and twanged their carillons of
    bronze
Sienna consonants embedded with the vowels *alexandrite, emerald* and *topaz.*

The topos of their discourse seemed to do with me and convoluted
    genealogy;
Wordy whorls and braids and skeins and spiral helices, unskeletoned from
    laminate geology—

How this one's slate-blue gaze is correspondent to another's new-born eyes;
Gentians, forget-me-nots, and cornflowers, diurnal in a heliotrope surmise.

Alexandrine tropes came gowling out like beagles, loped and unroped
On a snuffly Autumn. Nimrod followed after with his bold Arapahoes,

Who whooped and hollered in their unforked tongue. The trail was starred
    with
Myrrh and frankincense of Anno Domini; the Wise Men wisely paid their
    tariff.

A single star blazed at my window. Crepuscular, its acoustic perfume dims
And swells like flowers on the stanzaic-papered wall. Shipyard hymns

Then echoed from the East: gantry-clank and rivet-ranks, Six-County
    hexametric
Brackets, bulkheads, girders, beams, and stanchions; convocated and
    Titanic.

Leviathans of rope snarled out from ropeworks: disgorged hawsers, unkinkable lay,
Ratlines, S-twists, plaited halyards, Z-twists, catlines; all had their say.

Tobacco-scent and snuff breathed out in gouts of factory smoke like aromatic camomile;
Sheaves of brick-built mill-stacks glowered in the sulphur-mustard fog like campaniles.

The dim bronze noise of midnight-noon and Angelus then boomed and clinked in Latin
Conjugations; statues wore their shrouds of amaranth; the thurible chinked out its smoky patina.

I inhaled *amo, amas, amat* in quids of *pros* and *versus* and *Introibos*
Ad altare Dei; incomprehensibly to others, spoke in Irish. I slept through the Introit.

The enormous Monastery surrounded me with nave and architrave. Its ornate pulpit
Spoke to me in fleurs-de-lys of Purgatory. Its sacerdotal gaze became my pupil.

My pupil's nose was bathed in Pharaonic unguents of dope and glue.
Flimsy tissue-paper plans of aeroplanes unfolded whimsical ideas of the blue,

Where, unwound, the prop's elastic is unpropped and balsawood extends its wings
Into the hazardous azure of April. It whirrs into the realm of things.

Things are kinks that came in tubes; like glue or paint extruded, that became
A hieroglyphic alphabet. Incestuous in pyramids, Egyptians were becalmed.

I climbed into it, delved its passageways, its sepulchral interior, its things
     of kings
Embalmed; sarcophagi, whose perfume I exhumed in chancy versions of
     the *I-Ching.*

A chink of dawn was revelated by the window. Far-off cocks crowed
     crowingly
And I woke up, verbed and tensed with speaking English; I lisped the words
     so knowingly.

I love the as-yet morning, when no one's abroad, and I am like a postman
     on his walk,
Distributing strange messages and bills, and arbitrations with the world
     of talk:

I foot the snow and almost-dark. My shoes are crisp, and bite into the blue-
White firmament of pavement. My father holds my hand and goes blah-

Blah with me into the ceremonial dawn. I'm wearing tweed. The universe is
     Lent
And Easter is an unspun cerement, the gritty, knitty, tickly cloth of unspent

Time. I feel its warp and weft. Bobbins pirn and shuttle in Imperial
Typewriterspeak. I hit the keys. The ribbon-black clunks out the words in
     serial.

What comes next is next, and no one knows the *che sera* of it, but must allow
The Tipp-Ex present at the fingertips. Listen now: an angel whispers of the
     here-and-now.

The future looms into the mouth incessantly, gulped-at and unspoken;
Its guardian is intangible, but gives you hints and winks and nudges as its
     broken token.

I woke up blabbering and dumb with too much sleep. I rubbed my eyes
and ears.

I closed my eyes again and flittingly, forgetfully, I glimpsed the noise of
years.

APPARAT

Unparalyzed, the robot bomb-disposal expert inched and tacked across the
    mezzanine
As casually as someone to be barbered sits relaxing with a magazine.

It was using 'deep creep' and 'infinite hair', conversing in its base-of-two
    conundrum.
Its chips were bugged like all the toasters in the apparatchniks'
    condominium.

Turnbull twiddled with the radio controls. He twitched his robot's claws.
He felt the Mobile Ordinance Disposal Unit index through its dictionary of
    clues.

Umbilical, he was in the waiting room. Barberlike, he opened up his case of
    instruments.
He was beckoned by the realms of Nod. He entered in with incense and
    Byzantine vestments.

The smart bomb got the message and intoned the right liturgical analysis.
Latinate, they swapped explosive bits and pieces; they re-emerged in
    Nemesis.

DRUNK BOAT

after Arthur Rimbaud, 'Le bateau ivre'

As I glided down the lazy Meuse, I felt my punters had gone AWOL—
In fact, Arapahoes had captured them for target practice, nailing them to
    stakes. Oh hell,

I didn't give a damn. I didn't want a crew, nor loads of Belgian wheat, nor
    English cotton.
When the whoops and hollers died away their jobs were well forgotten.

Through the tug and zip of tides, more brain-deaf than an embryo, I
    bobbled;
Peninsulas, unmoored and islanded, were envious of my Babel-babble.

Storms presided at my maritime awakening. Like a cork I waltzed across the
    waves,
Which some call sailors' graveyards; but I despised their far-off, lighted
    enclaves.

As children think sour apples to be sweet, so the green sap swamped the
    planks
And washed away the rotgut and the puke, the rudder and the anchor-hanks.

I've been immersed, since then, in Sea Poetry, anthologized by stars,
As through the greenish Milky Way a corpse drifts downwards, clutching a
    corrupted spar;

When suddenly, those sapphire blues are purpled by Love's rusty red. No
    lyric
Alcohol, no Harp, can combat it, this slowly-pulsing, twilit panegyric.

I've known lightning, spouts, and undertows, maelstrom evenings that
     merge into Aurora's
Blossoming of doves. I've seen the Real Thing; others only get its aura.

I've seen the sun's demise, where seas unroll like violet, antique
Venetian blinds; dim spotlight, slatted by the backstage work of Ancient
     Greeks.

I dreamed the green, snow-dazzled night had risen up to kiss the seas'
Blue-yellow gaze, the million plankton eyes of phosphorescent argosies.

I followed then, for many months, the mad-cow waves of the Antipodes,
Oblivious to the Gospel of how Jesus calmed the waters, walking on his
     tippy-toes.

I bumped, you know, into the Floridas, incredible with pupil-flowers
And manatees, which panther-men had reined with rainbows and with
     Special Powers.

I saw a whole Leviathan rot slowly in the seething marsh, till it became
All grot and whalebone. Blind cataracts lurched into oubliettes, and were
     becalmed.

Glaciers and argent seas, pearly waves and firecoal skies! A tangled serpent-
     cordage
Hauled up from the Gulf, all black-perfumed and slabbered with a monster's
     verbiage!

I would have liked the children to have seen them: goldfish, singing-fish,
     John Dorys—
My unanchored ones, I'm cradled by the tidal flowers and lifted near to
     Paradise.

Sometimes, fed up with the Poles and Zones, the sea would give a briny sob and ease
Off me; show me, then, her vented shadow-flowers, and I'd be like a woman on her knees . . .

Peninsular, I juggled on my decks with mockingbirds and ostriches
And rambled on, until my frail lines caught another upsidedown, a drowned Australian.

Now see me, snarled-up in the reefs of bladderwrack, or thrown by the waterspout like craps
Into the birdless Æther, where Royal Navy men would slag my sea-drunk corpse—

Smoking, languorous in foggy violet, I breathed a fireglow patch into
The sky, whose azure trails of snot are snaffled by some Poets as an entrée—

Electromagnets, hoof-shaped and dynamic, drove the *Nautilus*. Black hippocampuses
Escorted it, while heatwaves drummed and blattered on the July campuses.

Me, I shivered: fifty leagues away, I heard the bumbling Behemoths and Scarabs;
Spider spinning in the emerald, I've drifted off the ancient parapets of Europe!

Sidereal archipelagoes I saw! Island skies, who madly welcomed the explorer;
O million starry birds, are these the endless nights you dream of for the Future?

I've whinged enough. Every dawn is desperate, every bitter sun. The moon's
   atrocious.
Let the keel split now, let me go down! For I am bloated, and the boat is
   stotious.

Had I some European water, it would be that cold, black puddle
Where a child once launched a paper boat—frail butterfly—into the dusk;
   and huddled

There, I am no more. O waves, you've bathed and cradled me and shaped
Me. I'll gaze no more at Blue Ensigns, nor merchantmen, nor the drawn
   blinds of prison-ships.

THE BRAIN OF EDWARD CARSON

They cracked the skull and watched its two halves creak apart, like the decks
Of some Byzantine trireme. The herringboned, zipped oars, the chains and
    shackles.
The bronze circuitry. The locks. The titanic, legal depositions of the cells.
The hammered rivets. The rivetted, internal gaze. The screws. The nails.
The caulked bulwarks. The slaves, embalmed in honeycomb prismatic.

Barbaric instruments inserted there, like hook and razor, iron picks
By which they will extrapolate its history: the bronze, eternal static
Of his right, uplifted hand. The left hand like a shield. The bolted-on, external
Eyes. The seraphic frown. The borders and the chains contained therein. The
    fraternal
Gaze of the Exclusive Brethren: orange and bruised purple, cataleptic.

The map of Ulster opened up, hexagonal and intricate, tectonic:
Its shifting plates were clunked and welded into place by laws Masonic.
The ladder and the rope. The codicils. The compasses by which they sail
Uncharted futures. The outstretched hand. The crown. The sash. The secret
    nail.
And then disintegration intervened, the brain eluded them: Sphinxlike,
    catatonic.

THE BALLAD OF HMS BELFAST

On the first of April *Belfast* disengaged her moorings and sailed away
From old Bel*fast*. Sealed orders held our destination, somewhere in the Briny
    Say.

Our crew of Jacks was aromatic with tobacco-twist and alcoholic
Reekings from the night before. Both Catestants and Protholics,

We were tarry-breeked and pig-tailed, and sailed beneath the White Ensign;
We loved each other nautically, though most landlubbers thought we were
    insane.

We were full-rigged like the *Beagle*, piston-driven like the *Enterprise*
Express; each system was a back-up for the other, auxiliarizing verse with
    prose.

Our engines ticked and tacked us up the Lough, cranks and link-pins, cross-
    rods
Working ninety to the dozen; our shrouds and ratlines rattled like a cross-
    roads

Dance, while swivels, hook blocks, cleats, and fiddles jigged their semi-
    colons
On the staves. We staggered up the rigging like a bunch of demi-golems,

Tipsy still, and dreamed of underdecks—state-rooms, crystal chandeliers,
And saloon bars—until we got to gulp the ozone; then we swayed like
    gondoliers

Above the aqua. We gazed at imperceptible horizons, where amethyst
Dims into blue, and pondered them again that night, before the mast.

Some sang of Zanzibar and Montalban, and others of the lands
    unascertained
On maps; we entertained the Phoenix and the Unicorn, till we were grogged
    and concertina'ed.

We've been immersed, since then, in cruises to the Podes and Antipodes;
The dolphin and the flying fish would chaperone us like aquatic aunties

In their second, mermaid childhood, till we ourselves felt neither fish nor
    flesh, but
Breathed through gills of rum and brandy. We'd flounder on the randy decks
    like halibut.

Then our Captain would emerge to scold us from his three days'
    incommunicado
And promenaded on the poop-deck, sashed and epauletted like a grand
    Mikado

To bribe us with the Future: new Empires, Realms of Gold, and precious ore
Unheard-of since the days of Homer: we'd boldly go where none had gone
    before.

Ice to Archangel, tea to China, coals to Tyne: such would be our cargo.
We'd confound the speculators' markets and their exchequered, logical
    embargo.

Then were we like the *Nautilus* that trawls the vast and purple catacomb
For cloudy shipwrecks, settled in their off-the-beam, intractable aplomb.

Electric denizens glide through the Pisan masts, flickering their Pisces'
    lumière;
We regard them with a Cyclops eye, from our bathyscope beneath *la mer*.

Scattered cutlery and dinner-services lie, hugger-mugger, on the murky
floor.
An empty deckchair yawns and undulates its awning like a semaphore.

Our rising bubble then went *bloop, bloop* till it burst the swaying
windowpane;
Unfathomed from the cobalt deep, we breathed the broad Pacific once again.

Kon-Tiki-like, we'd drift for days, abandoning ourselves to all the elements,
Guided only by the aromatic coconut, till the wind brought us the scent of
lemons—

Then we'd disembark at Vallambroso or Gibraltar to explore the bars;
Adorned in sequin-scales, we glimmered phosphorescently like stars

That crowd innumerably in midnight harbours. O olive-dark interior,
All splashed with salt and wine! Havana gloom within the humidor!

The atmosphere dripped heavy with the oil of anchovies, tobacco smoke,
and chaw;
We grew languorous with grass and opium and *kif*, the very best of draw,

And sprawled in urinous piazzas; slept until the foghorn trump of Gabriel.
We woke, and rubbed our eyes, half-gargled still with braggadocio and
garble.

And then the smell of docks and ropeworks. Horse-dung. The tolling of the
Albert clock.
Its Pisan slant. The whirring of its ratchets. Then everything began to click:

I lay bound in iron chains, alone, my *aisling* gone, my sentence passed.
Grey Belfast dawn illuminated me, on board the prison-ship Bel*fast*.

THE ALBATROSS

after Charles Baudelaire, 'L'albatros'

Often, for a gag, the Jack Tars like to catch an albatross, Aviator
Of the high seas who, following the navy, wants to be its Avatar.

But they slap him, Emperor of Blue, down on the salty planks. They taunt
   him.
Spat at, tripped up, his wings creak helplessly like oars, and haunt him.

This wingèd voyager, now bedraggled, ugly, awkward, how pathetic!
Someone pokes a pipe into his mouth, and someone else who mimics him
   is paralytic.

The Poet's like that Prince of Clouds, who soars above the archer and the
   hurricane: Great Auk
Brought down to earth, his gawky, gorgeous wings impede his walk.

A

Invisible to radar, *Stealth* glided through their retina of sweep and dot.
No bleep appeared to register its Alpha wing. The watchers were asleep,
   or not.

An Ampoule-bomb lay Ampere-wired-up in it, waiting for its primal sec-
Ond, like its embryonic *A* becoming *Be*. It wanted flash and Instamatic.

Its crew is snorkelled into oxygen, and getting high as kites. Its eagle eye
Zooms in and out across the infra-red. Its map is virtual reality:

O porcelain metropolis, inlaid with palaces of majuscule Baroque
And Trojan *equus* statues; fountains, spices, frozen music, gardens, oranges
   from Maroc!

I put my feet into the crew's shoes, my hands into their gloves, and felt the
   chill
Of borrowed armour. My *a priori* gauntlet twitched and hit the button: *Kill*.

D

Whoever takes an arrow to this bow will really feel the slippery sap
Of the freshly-peeled sally rod and the tensile spring of the future slap

Of the string, all imaginary targets riddled through with past plu-
Perfect hits and misses; the lucky shot of two birds skewered in the perfect
    blue.

All thumbs and fingers tweezerlike, I unbarbed his fletcher's herringbone,
Like I unstuck the hoops and loops of the Velcro Celtic Twilight Zone.

I unzipped it open, and so witnessed the opposing oars of quinquereme
And decked-out trireme, how they rowed majestically into Byzantium:

A shower of arrows welcomed them like needles to a magnet, like the whole
Assault of future into present, the way that the South attracts the North
    pole.

G

His hand had been clamped in a G-clamp to the Black & Decker workbench.
Claw-head hammers, pincers, lost-head nails: they said it was the work of
   Untermensch.

Meanwhile, G-men trawled the underworld with darkened retinas and
   double-
Breasted trench coats. Shook hands at funerals, saying, *Sorry for your trouble.*

Meanwhile, bugs proliferated all across the city: gnats, gads, gargle-flies
   and gall-flies
Spawned from entomology of G; they laid their eggs in gigabits in databanks
   and files of lies.

Meanwhile, they took in the buzz in the bar through the radio-blue-bottle-
   lens,
As 'Black' told 'Decker' what had really *sotto voce* happened. The bits they
   got made sense:

Meanwhile, his hand has been clamped in the jaws of a vice to the workbench.
X and Y are dissecting the best approach to the work. X picks up a wrench.

H

The Powers-that-Be decreed that from the — of ——— the sausage rolls, for reasons
Of security, would be contracted to a different firm. They gave the prisoners no reasons.

The prisoners complained. We cannot reproduce his actual words here, since their spokesman is alleged
To be a sub-commander of a movement deemed to be illegal.

An actor spoke for him in almost-perfect lip-sync: *It's not the quality*
We're giving off about. Just that it seems they're getting smaller. We're talking quantity.

His 'Belfast' accent wasn't West enough. Is the H in H-Block *aitch* or *haitch*?
Does it matter? *What we have we hold? Our day will come?* Give or take an inch?

Well, give an inch and someone takes an effing mile. Every thing is in the ways
You say them. Like, the prison that we call Long Kesh is to the Powers-that-Be *The Maze*.

K

K is the leader of the empty orchestra of karaoke.
K is the conductor on the wrong bus that you took today and landed you in
    yesterday

Where everything was skew. The rainbow colours were all out of kilter,
Like oil had leaked out all over the road from a dropped and broken philtre.

There, no one wanted to be recognized, and walked around in wrap-round
Polaroids. There was Semtex in the Maxwell House, and twenty shillings in
    the pound.

K came into it again, with the sidelong, armed stance of a Pharaoh.
He took my kopek, docked it with two holes, and told me it was time to go.

All the motor cars were black. I got behind the wheel of one. It worked OK.
Welder's sparks zipped from the trolley. The radio was playing karaoke.

O

The tea-cup stain on the white damask tablecloth was not quite perfect.
    Never-
Theless, I'd set my cup exactly on it, like it was a stain-remover.

I sipped the rim with palatable lip. I drank the steaming liquor up.
My granny then would read my future from the tea-leaves' leavings in the
    cup.

I stared into enormous china O and saw its every centrifugal flaw,
The tiny bobbles glazed in its interior of Delphic oracle. I yawned

Into its incandescent blaze of vowel like the cool of dudes in black fedoras
At high noon; trigger-fingered, shadowless, they walked beneath sombreros.

They stopped me inadvertently and asked for my identity. I did not know
Until the mouth of a gun was pressed against my forehead, and I felt its O.

Z

The ultimate buzz is the sound of sleep or of bees, or the slalom I'll
Make through the dark pines of a little-known Alp on my snowmobile.

You will hear me fading and droning towards you from the valley next
To one, for I have miles to go: when I deliver all the letters, that's the text.

The canvas sack on my back reminds me I am in the archaic footprints
Of my postman father. I criss and cross the zigzag precedents.

Snow is falling fast, my parallels already blurring on the mountainside,
But I am flying towards you through the stars on skis of Astroglide.

In the morning you will open up the envelope. You will get whatever
Message is inside. It is for all time. Its postmark is 'The Twelfth of Never'.

ME AND MY COUSIN

after the Romanian of Stefan Augustin Doinas

'As for the Archaeopteryx—for such I thought it might have been—
  I hopped on to its neck.
It turned out to be an alabaster blue. Its name was really Roc.

Syllables of evening stars becoming Lucifers dropped from its beak;
Three deep infernos, funnel-grey, were born within its awful look.

Over and above the stratosphere I flew; from noon to dewy eve I whirled,
Till I glanced down and noticed it had laid an egg. The egg was called The
  World.'

'Yes,' my cousin said, 'mind you, this Dodo—Roc or Archaeopteryx—does
  not exist.'
'No, it don't,' I answered, as I grappled with its neck, 'I know it don't exist.'

JACTA EST ALEA

It was one of those puzzling necks of the wood where the South was in the
    North, the way
The double cross in a jigsaw loops into its matrix, like the border was a *clef*

With arbitrary teeth indented in it. Here, it cut clean across the plastic
Lounge of The Half-Way House; my heart lay in the Republic

While my head was in the Six, or so I was inclined. You know that drinker's
Angle, elbow-propped, knuckles to his brow like one of the Great Thinkers?

He's staring at my throat in the Power's mirror, debating whether
He should open up a lexicon with me: the price of beer or steers, the
    weather.

We end up talking about talk. We stagger on the frontier. He is pro. I am con.
Siamese-like, drunken, inextricable, we wade into the Rubicon.

GRAECUM EST: NON LEGITUR

The fly made an audible syzygy as it dive-bombed through the dormer
And made a rendezvous with this, the page I'm writing on. It was its karma.

This tsetse was a Greek to me, making wishy-washy gestures with its hands
And feet. I made to brush it off, before it vaulted off into a handstand

Ceiling-corner of the room. It dithered over to the chandelier-flex
And buzzed around it upside down in a stunt-plane Camel helix.

The landing-page approached my craft as I began to think again. The candle
    guttered.
My enormous hand was writing on the wall. The words began to stutter

As the quill ran out. *Syzygy*: His dizzy Nibs was back. I took on board more
    ink.
He staggered horse-like towards the blue blot I'd just dropped. Then he
    began to drink.

SIEGE

after Stefan Augustin Doinas

The fortress balanced on a lance-tip. Unseen army. The wells were clogged,
The smoke kept low. We caught the double-headed eagle and we ate its
   mystagogue.

Epidemics came and went. Familiar atavistic ghosts kept firing arrows
From the parapets into the world beyond. Nothing. Only the stars

In the wound in the side of the god. Then treason struck at midnight and
   the gate
Capitulated. Cowards kow-towed. Nobody. The dazzling pirate

Moon broke out. Still nobody. Afflicted by a strange disease of sundered
Windows, we weep eternities of blood. There's nobody. But we, we have
   surrendered.

JULIET

I met him in Verona Market, fingering the oranges and the greens.
He seemed interested in local produce. We were into Kings and Queens.

I bought a bunch of thyme. He bought rue. Our hands touched. I was
    contagious to a Montague,
And the grand piazza was pizzaz with heraldry emblazoned in a rendezvous

Of factions: oriflammes and banderoles, standards, swallowtails and
    bannerettes,
All fluttering with shamrocks, roses, thistles, high above the parapets

Where guzzling trumpeters tilted trumpets to their lips like bottles full of
    Coke
Or dope-imbibers gazing at the ceiling, relishing their skywriting smoke.

We called the song they played 'Our Song'. I thought together we would be,
    perhaps.
But the Montagues put on their cloaks, the Capulets put on their caps.

KILO

The *Sûreté* had guaranteed the operation would be covert, low-key,
Hunky-dory, under wraps, each detail okey-dokey as synecdoche;

You recognize the Citröen by its wheels? That's what I mean: the part
Denotes the smoky whole, especially when played by Humphrey Bogart.

A car-klaxon blew a foggy Gauloise note of pianissimo accordion bass
Droned out across an empty ballroom floor; the dancers were in hyperspace.

The foreign freighter creaked its starry moorings. Frogmen swam up
    through a galaxy,
Synchronized like watches. The rendezvous would happen in a Falls Road
    taxi.

Paki Black, Red Leb, and Acupulco Gold: dogs sniffed the aromatic rainbow.
Maigret blew a cloud of briar smoke and spoke: *Lo-Ki? Kilo? OK! KO!*

OSCAR

I held the figurine aloft, revelling in my actor's gravestone smile;
I boldly faced an orchestra of flash, as paparazzi packed the aisle.

I thanked everyone: all those who'd made it possible for me to be,
Down to the midwife and my grade-school teacher; my analyst; the
    Committee;

Not forgetting William Shakespeare, who had writ the script on vellum,
Nor the born anachronist director, who had set it in the *ante bellum*—

The way he saw it, Hamlet was a kind of Southern dude who chewed
    cheroots.
He wanted Vivien to play Ophelia Leigh. The uncle was a *putz*.

So, everybody, give a big hand to *All Our Yesterdays*, this apron weft
And warp of life we strut upon a brief while, till *All exeunt, stage left*.

ROMEO

Romeo was not built in a day, not to speak of Romulus or Remus—
Cain and Abel—why Protestants are called Billy—and Catholics are Seamus.

It took a school lab labyrinth of history to produce these garbled notes
In careful fountain-pen. The arrowed maps of North and South, the essays
    filled with quotes:

The emptied jam-jar full of frogspawn, blooping on the window sill;
The tapioca of school meals; the sandwiches of squashed Norwegian sild;

John West in his sou'wester; Vesta matches in their yellow box, the Swift in
    blue;
The Orange lily and the Shamrock green; shades of Capulet and Montague—

It's all a tangled tagliatelle linguini Veronese that I'm trying to unravel
From its strands of DNA and language. Perhaps I need a spirit level.

X-RAY

The faces of the disappeared in blown-up, blurred wedding photographs;
The bombing of the Opera House; my lost wall map of Belfast; the pikestaffs

Spiked with rebels' decomposing heads; the long-since rotted hempen rope;
The razor-wire; the Confidential Telephone; the walls that talk of FUCK THE
    POPE;

The dragons' teeth; the look-out towers; the body politic surveillances;
The terrorist, the might-have-been of half-forgotten, long-abandoned chances:

All these are nothing to the blinks and blanks of night's inscrutable eternity, which stars
    which stars
The Northern sky with camp fire palimpsests of ancient wars;

Or these are nothing to the cerebral activity of any one of us who sets in train
These zigzags, or the brain cells decomposing in some rebel brain.

THE SLEEPER IN THE VALLEY

after Arthur Rimbaud, 'Le dormeur du val'

It's a greeny dip where a crazy guggling rill
Makes silver tatters of itself among the grass;
Where the sun pours down from the wild high mountain-sill;
It foams with light like bubbles in a champagne glass.

A soldier sleeps there, tousle-headed, mouth agape,
The nape of his neck drenched in cool blue watercress;
He's sprawled on the grass beneath a seething cloudscape,
Pale in the dew which oozes like juice from a wine press.

His boots among the lilies, he lies sleeping, smiling
The smile of a sick child, cradle-head reclining.
Nature, rock him in your bosom warmly: he is cold.

No mortal smell assails his nostrils now; he's fast
Asleep, left hand on his heart. He's found peace at last.
Come closer: there, in his right side, are two red holes.

ON THE ROAD

after Arthur Rimbaud, 'Ma bohème'

Thumbs hitched into my holey pockets, off I hiked
In my has-been-through-the-wars ex-Army greatcoat;
Under your blue skies, O muse, you took me on your bike;
I loved the way in which we spun in perfect rote.

My trousers had a hole as big as any arse,
And I became a dwarf who scatters rhymes along
The Milky Way. In the Great Bear I sang my song,
As huge stars shivered in the rustling universe.

And I listened to their dew of blue September
Evenings fall on me, like Long Ago remembered
In the first sip of a cool green bubble-beaded wine;

I strummed the black elastic of my tattered boot
Held to my heart like youthful violin or lute,
A veritable pop star of the awful rhyme.

AT THE SIGN OF THE SWAN

after Stéphane Mallarmé, 'Le vierge, le vivace et le bel aujourd'hui . . .'

The beautiful today, untouched by human hand,
Swings towards us with a stagger of its drunken wing
To crash the frozen lake as cold as anything,
Ghosted by the glacial distances it never spanned!

A fabled swan the image of an ampersand
Is mute, for all his freed necessity to sing
His icy habitat of winter's fosterling,
Where dim suns yawned their tedium across the land.

His whole neck shudders off this agony of white
Impressed upon him by the spacey ambient light,
But not the Earth, where he's incapable of flight.

Beautiful ghost, condemned by his own brilliant line,
Engraved within a pond of icy crystallite,
He maintains the useless exile of a Swan, or sign.

THE TOMB OF CHARLES BAUDELAIRE

after Stéphane Mallarmé, 'Le tombeau de Charles Baudelaire'

Through the slimy open grating of a storm-drain
The entombed temple slobbers muck and rubies,
Abominable as the dog-god Anubis
Whose muzzle blazes with a howl of savage pain.

It's like the new gas of an odorous campaign
Against the dark, illuminating our disease—
Immortal whore as old as Mephistopheles
Who flits from lamp to lamp beside the foggy Seine.

What wreaths, in cities of no votive evenings,
Can offer benediction to us, as she flings
Herself in vain against a marble Baudelaire?

As trembling veils of light absent her from our gaze,
She has become his deadly-nightshade-poisoned air
That we must breathe, although we perish in its maze.

RAINY LIAISONS

after Charles Baudelaire, 'Spleen'

Here comes Mr Rainy Month again, to vent his spleen
Across the city, lashing elemental squalls
On mortals in the fog-enshrouded urban scene,
And pale denizens behind cemetery walls.

My cat prowls round like she was high on mescaline
In her electric mangy fur. She meows and wauls,
And outside, in the gutter of the could-have-been,
Some miserable poet's ghost complains and crawls.

Church bells dong on slowly through the thickening gloom:
A hissing log; the clock's asthmatic pendulum.
Meanwhile, in a used pack of dirty playing cards,

Discarded by some poxy whore, the Queen of Spades
And greasy Jack of Hearts discuss their defunct trades
Of love: rainy liaisons of the dark back yards.

COEXISTENCES

after Charles Baudelaire, 'Correspondances'

Nature is a temple, in which vibrant columns
Sometimes utter green, confused auxiliaries of leaf
And verb; Man stumbles through the Forest of Belief,
Which watches him with pupils of its hidden sanctums.

Like blue extended husky echoes from away
Far off, which cloud together in the inner or
The outer space of constellations in a mirror,
Shimmery perfumes, colours, sounds, all shift and sway.

There are communiqués of scent which bloom like oboe
Music on the skin of babies, or the verdant
Noise of meadows; others, like a smoky flambeau,

Light the vast expansiveness of things awry and slant
Which drift together in an amber incense musk
And chant their holy slogans in the ambient dusk.

ADELAIDE HALT

There is a smell of coal and iron. Black lumps
Of ballast gleam between the rained-on parallels.
I hear a blast of steam. Smoke floats across the dumps.
The platform trembles with the far-off decibels

Emitted by the almost imminent express.
Seventeen long coaches shimmered by to Dublin:
A blur of diners, drinkers, couples playing chess.
A sudden interim, then nitroglycerin

Booms from the quarry where they're mining basalt.
A gable wall says FUCK THE POPE. I feel exposed,
As fragile as a model galleon carved from salt.

Overhead, the adenoidal honking of wild geese.
Adelaide? The name? A city or a girl, who knows?
There is a drink called Hope, a cigarette called Peace.

THE BLUE SHAMROCK

Now they rehearse their ancient music on the harp,
And blow blue music from the bonsai bamboo flute,
The President is talking to the ancient carp
Which swims in green gloom in the Pisces Institute.

Like a ventriloquist she reads its silent lip,
Interpreting the gnomic bubbles of its word,
Which bloop like quavers of a psychedelic trip,
Or nimble foldings of the origami bird.

As a surface of the pool begins to ripple
She undoes the couplets of her blue kimono,
And as King Fish comes up she offers him her nipple.

This, Dear Sir, is when the spirit enters matter
Or, as a master summarized it long ago,
Old pond: a frog jumps in: the sound of water.

SAYERS, OR, BOTH SAW WONDERS

We lay down in the Forest of Forget-me-not;
You slept, and from your open lips an Admiral
Emerged as if out for a daily ramble,
Quivering its wings as vivid as a Rorschach blot.

It crept down you, over a stream and through the rye
Into an open socket of an equine skull,
To wander for a lull within that Trojan hull,
Before it crawled out from the other empty eye.

Then it returned into your mouth the way it went.
You woke, and told me of your labyrinthine dream:
The highway—river—palace—rooms of vast extent—

'It looks as if the soul's a butterfly,' I said,
'Yet many who've elaborated on this theme
Have never seen the inside of a horse's head.'

SPRAYING THE POTATOES

Knapsack-sprayer on my back, I marched the drills
Of blossoming potatoes—Kerr's Pinks in a frivelled blue,
The Arran Banners wearing white. July was due,
A haze of copper sulphate on the far-off hills.

The bronze noon air was drowsy, unguent as glue.
As I bent over the big oil-drum for a refill
I heard the axle-roll of a rut-locked tumbril.
It might have come from God-knows-where, or out of the blue.

A verdant man was cuffed and shackled to its bed.
Fourteen troopers rode beside, all dressed in red.
It took them a minute to string him up from the oak tree.

I watched him swing in his Derry green for hours and hours,
His popping eyes of apoplectic liberty
That blindly scanned the blue and white potato flowers.

1798

I met her in the garden where the poppies grow,
Quite over-canopied with luscious woodbine,
And her cheeks were like roses, or blood dropped on snow;
Her pallid lips were red with Papal Spanish wine.

Lulled in these wild flowers, with dance and delight,
I took my opportunity, and grasped her hand.
She then disclosed the eyelids of her second sight,
And prophesied that I'd forsake my native land.

Before I could protest she put her mouth to mine
And sucked the broken English from my Gaelic tongue.
She wound me in her briary arms of eglantine.

Two centuries have gone, yet she and I abide
Like emblems of a rebel song no longer sung,
Or snowy blossoms drifting down the mountainside.

HEART OF OAK

Coming to in the Twelfth Meadow, I was still
Woozy with whatever it was had happened me.
I felt like Ahab's Herman Melville,
Regurgitated by a monster of cetacean pedigree.

It'd seemed I'd swum into my own enormous maw
Some months ago. I'd made the ribcage my abode:
Vaulted hall wherein a swallowed galleon creaked and yawed,
And labyrinths of gloomy light were blue as woad.

In this realm, everything was fitted to my needs:
The Captain's library, his map and compasses,
His davenport, at which I wrote these many screeds,

His microscope, his grand *pianoforte*—
Only the guns and shot were completely useless.
I left them there to rust when I regained my liberty.

BANNERS

For all that died from shot and sword, more died of disease:
Plagues, dysentery, miasmas, suppurating grot
Beyond the non-existent doctors' expertise.
Some were given military burials, others not.

Starved with cold, *La Grande Armée*, like dots in domino,
Stumbled through Borovsk and Vereya to Mojaisk,
To recross the battlefield of Borodino:
For this enormous freezing tomb, no obelisk,

But the ground ploughed by cannonballs, harrowed by lances,
Littered with cuirasses, wheels, rags, and thirty thousand
Bodies with no eyes who devoured our glances.

As we passed them we almost took them for our foes,
And for a moment I thought of dear old Ireland:
Fields of corpses plentiful as dug potatoes.

FINDING THE OX

A Zen warrior searches for inner peace.
His bow is like a harp, that he might twang its string
In lonely combat with himself, and so release
The arrow of desire. An archer should want nothing.

His is the blue music of what is happening.
His sword rings true. Its many lives of hammered steel
Were there before him, and he trusts its weighty swing.
He knows the rallentando of a roulette wheel,

Or red leaves floating in a stream of eau de nil,
Bisected by a showy rival blade, while his
The leaves avoided. He's the opposite of zeal.

When he aims at the bull he closes his eyes.
Sometimes he hits it dead-on with a mighty whizz.
Sometimes he's way off target, which is no surprise.

GREEN TEA

I saw a magnified red dot on a white field.
I saw the terraces and pyramids of salt.
I saw a towering mushroom cloud of cobalt.
I made sure my papers had been signed and sealed.

The writing everywhere on walls illegible to me.
The faces in the crowds unrecognizable.
The labyrinth to which I hadn't got the key.
Investing in the Zen is inadvisable.

Zeno made a gesture with his disembodied hand.
A landscape wafted into being from his brush.
The flow of water is represented by sand.

If anything, I think I drank too much green tea.
The snows of Fujiyama had all turned to slush.
Hibernia beckoned from across the blue sea.

TWELFTH DAY

Drunk as a bee that bumbles from deep in the bell
Of a Fairy's Thimble, in a heat-dazed summer meadow,
We sprawled as if we listened to a radio
Which broadcast nothing except insect decibel.

The volume of the field was many atmospheres
Of crawling, chittering, tiny Arcadians,
To whom teeming minutes might be days, and hours years.
In this vast universe we were the aliens.

Every flower we saw, each stalk, was colonized
By troops of little fellows marching up and down
In perfect harmony, as if transistorized.

I went to pinch one 'twixt my index and my thumb
When someone turned the volume up in Portadown,
And then I heard the whole field pulsing like an Orange drum.

SPENSER'S IRELAND

Rakehelly horseboys, kernes, gallowglasses, carrows,
Bards, captains, rapparees, their forward womenfolk,
Swords, dice, whiskey, chess, harps, word-hoards, bows and arrows:
All are hid within the foldings of their Irish cloak.

Fit house for an outlaw, meet bed for a rebel,
This whore's wardrobe is convenient for a thief;
And when it freezes it becomes his tabernacle,
In whose snug he finds Hibernian relief.

Then there is this big thick bush of hair hanging down
Over their eyes—a *glib*, they call it in their spake;
They do not recognize the power of the Crown.

At the drop of a hat they are wont to vanish
Into deep dark woods. Forever on the make,
They drink and talk too much. Not all of it is gibberish.

PLANXTY MISS DICKINSON

I've seen a narrow fellow tumbling through the rye—
You could mistake him for a whiskery ear
Of it, such is his camouflage of elfin gear;
And his whispery voice is like a mimicry.

Sometimes I see him casting a gossamer thread
To catch a butterfly and hitch a ride on it,
To waltz about above me like a drunken Zed,
Then vanish in a twinkling from my ambit.

And the drift of his speech is sometimes difficult to get,
Being wavery like blown grass, but I know some things
About its complicated phatic etiquette.

For instance, they've no way of saying yes, nor no,
For all their words and deeds are borne on viewless wings
Into the windblown ambiguity of snow.

THE DISPLAY CASE

Last night Hibernia appeared to me in regal frame,
In Creggan churchyard where I lay near dead from drink.
'Take down these words,' she said, 'that all might know my claim.'
I opened up a vein and drew my blood for ink—

I'd no accoutrements of writing, save the knife;
The pen she gave me was a feather from her plumage,
And my arm the parchment where I'd sign away my life.
'You seem,' she says, 'to have a problem with the language,

'Since you've abandoned it for lisping English,
Scribbling poems in it exclusively, or so I'm told.
Turncoat interpreter, you wonder why I languish?'

Her full speech is tattooed for all time on my mummied arm,
A relic some girl salvaged from the scaffold
Where they quartered me. *God keep the Irish from all harm!*

THE AMBASSADORS

Here, let me take you down to the Poppy Fields.
You scent them? They are almost bended for picking.
Here strut the soldiers in their ceremonial shields.
You list them? They are all alive and ticking.

As you can see the shields are furnished like mirrors
To reflect and shimmer the wavery poppies,
Like bandaged veterans of former bloody wars
For, as you know, all businesses need copies.

I hope I'm not being indiscreet when I reveal
That our President has many body-doubles:
Who knows what is what within the car of armoured steel?

You know, our two states could stand in each other's stead.
Excuse me, Sir, I am sorry for your troubles.
It seems you've got a poppy bullet in your head.

BELFAST

east

beyond the yellow
shipyard cranes

a blackbird whistles
in a whin bush

west

beside the motorway
a black taxi

rusts in a field
of blue thistles

BREAKING

red alert
car parked

in a red
zone

about to

disintegrate
it's

oh

so quiet

you can
almost

hear it rust

NEWS

alarms
shrill

lights
flash

as dust
clears

above
the paper

shop

The Belfast Telegraph
sign reads

      fast   *rap*

GALLIPOLI

Take sheds and stalls from Billingsgate,
glittering with scaling-knives and fish,
the tumbledown outhouses of English farmers' yards
that reek of dung and straw, and horses
cantering the mewsy lanes of Dublin;

take an Irish landlord's ruinous estate,
elaborate pagodas from a Chinese Delftware dish
where fishes fly through shrouds and sails and yards
of leaking ballast-laden junks bound for Benares
in search of bucket-loads of tea as black as tin;

take a dirty gutter from a backstreet in Boulogne,
where shops and houses teeter so their pitched roofs meet,
some chimney stacks as tall as those in Sheffield
or Irish round towers,
smoking like a fleet of British ironclad destroyers;

take the garlic-oregano-tainted arcades of Bologna,
linguini-twists of souks and smells of rotten meat,
as labyrinthine as the rifle-factories of Springfield,
or the tenements deployed by bad employers
who sit in parlours doing business drinking Power's;

then populate this slum with Cypriot and Turk,
Armenians and Arabs, British riflemen
and French Zouaves, camel-drivers, officers, and sailors,
sappers, miners, Nubian slaves, Greek money-changers,
plus interpreters who do not know the lingo;

dress them in turbans, shawls of fancy needlework,
fedoras, fezzes, sashes, shirts of fine Valenciennes,
boleros, pantaloons designed by jobbing tailors,
knickerbockers of the ostrich and the pink flamingo,
sans-culottes, and outfits even stranger;

requisition slaughterhouses for the troops,
and stalls with sherbet, lemonade, and rancid lard for sale,
a temporary hospital or two, a jail,
a stagnant harbour redolent with cholera,
and open sewers running down the streets;

let the staple diet be green cantaloupes
swarming with flies washed down with sour wine,
accompanied by the Byzantine
jangly music of the cithara
and the multilingual squawks of parakeets—

O landscape riddled with the diamond mines of Kimberley,
and all the oubliettes of Trebizond,
where opium-smokers doze among the Persian rugs,
and spies and whores in dim-lit snugs
discuss the failing prowess of the Allied powers,

where prowling dogs sniff for offal beyond
the stench of pulped plums and apricots,
from which is distilled the brandy they call 'grape-shot',
and soldiers lie dead or drunk among the crushed flowers—
I have not even begun to describe Gallipoli.

BREATH

watching
helicopter

gone

there's a
clear blue

space

above
my head

I feel

rinsed

clean

you know
that quiet

when the
washing-machine

stops
shuddering

SKIP

I'm writing
this

in a black flip-
top police

notebook
I gleaned

from the
bomb-

damage
of Her Majesty's

Stationery Office

WAR

Sergeant Talbot
had his head

swept off
by a

round-shot

yet for half
a furlong

more

the body kept
the saddle

horse and rider
charging on

regardless

FRAGMENT

from a piece of
the Tupperware
lunchbox that held

the wiring

they could tell
the bombmaker wore
Marigold rubber gloves

SEDAN

Cavalry men asleep
on their horses' necks.
In the fields, heaps

of sodden troops,
the countryside charming,
covered with rich crops,

but trampled
underfoot, vines and hops
swept aside by the flood

of battle, the apples blasted
from the trees, scattered
like grape-shot.

Gutted knapsacks, boots,
cavalry caps, jackets, swords,
mess-tins, bayonets,

canteens, firelocks, tunics,
sabres, epaulettes,
overturned baggage cars,

dead horses
with their legs in the air,
scattered everywhere,

dead bodies,
mostly of Turcos and Zouaves,
picked over by pickpockets,

one of them staggering
under a huge load of gold
watches and teeth.

Hands hanging in the trees
in lieu of fruit,
trunkless legs at their feet.

I will never forget one man
whose head rested
on a heap of apples,

his knees drawn up
to his chin, his eyes wide
open, seeming to inspect

the head of a Turco or Zouave
which, blown clean off,
lay like a cannonball in his lap.

What debris a ruined empire
leaves behind it!
By the time I reached Sedan

with my crippled horse
it was almost impossible
to ride through the streets

without treading on
bayonets and sabres, heaps
of shakos, thousands

of imperial eagles
torn off infantry caps,
or knocking into stooks

of musketry and pikes.
I thought of Sevastopol,
mirrors in fragments

on the floors, beds
ripped open, feathers
in the rooms a foot deep,

chairs, sofas, bedsteads,
bookcases, picture frames,
images of saints, shoes, boots,

bottles, physic jars,
the walls and doors
hacked with swords,

even the bomb shelters
ransacked, though in one dugout
I found a music book

with a woman's name
in it, and a canary bird,
and a vase of wild flowers.

ON THE CONTRARY

It's because we were brought up to lead double lives, you said.
You were lying next to me, both of us verging on sleep.

We always had to withhold ourselves from the other side,
guarding our tongues lest we answer to their outspoken laws.

And so we lost ourselves in the dark forest of language
believing in nothing which might not be governed by touch

or taste, the apple bursting indescribably with juice
against the roof of the mouth, or the clean cold smell of skin.

As our promise was never to be betrayed by our words
so we became our own shadowy police watching us,

as loaded the long goods train clanks slowly towards Dublin
we hear the shriek in the night from across the trip-wired fields,

as the searchlight trawls across the bedroom window you turn
towards me speechlessly and we look into each other's eyes.

REVOLUTION

Then I would try to separate the grain from the chaff of
helicopter noise as it hovered above on my house.

This was back in the late Sixties, I didn't know you then.
Later I'd picture you in an apartment in Paris.

You'd be watching riot police and students on TV,
banners and barbed wire unfurling across the boulevards

and the air thick with stones. The helicopters came later
within earshot grinding the sound bites into vocables.

I felt I had a malfunctioning cochlear implant,
that someone I didn't know was watching me from on high.

The picture would break up into unreadable pixels.
I'd imagine putting my lips to the door of your ear

as I held the conch you brought back from Ithaca to mine,
listening to shells becoming shingle, and shingle sand.

BIRTHRIGHT

You ask what's in a name? Where I come from it tells you where
you're from, I said, whether this allegiance or the other.

But you can always change your name, you said. Not where I'm from,
I said, that would be considered a collaboration.

Or rather, an apostasy. The act of a turncoat.
In any case, they'll find you out no matter what, for there

are other indicators of identity. Such as?
you said. Colour and cut of clothes, I said, the way you talk

and what you talk about, the way you walk, your stance, or how
you look askance, the set and colour of your eyes and hair.

Just look at you, you said, you're talking through your hat. Look at
what you're wearing, that good Protestant Harris tweed jacket.

The black serge waistcoat a linen broker might have cast off.
The grandfather shirt no grandfather of yours ever wore.

THE SHADOW

You know how you know when someone's telling lies? you said. They
get their story right every time, down to the last word.

Whereas when they tell the truth it's never the same twice. They
reformulate. The day in question and whatever passed

between them and the other can be seen so many ways,
the way they sometimes ask themselves if it happened at all.

All this was *à propos* of your first time in East Berlin.
The Wall was not long down. It was Easter 1990,

you found yourself in a place in Herman-Hesse-Strasse.
You were alone in the dining room one evening, reading

The Glass Bead Game over *Bierwurst*, sauerkraut and a draught beer,
when the middle-aged waiter approached you from the shadows.

Bitte, he said; may I? You gestured towards an empty chair.
You wouldn't remember how the talk took the turn it did,

but however it happened his life began to come out.
He'd set up two schnapps by then. He'd been in the Stasi once.

The lie is memorized, the truth is remembered, he said.
I learned that early on in their school before I became

interrogator. That was after I learned to listen
in. They played many tapes of many stories, some true, some

false. I was asked to identify which was which, and where
the conversations might have taken place, whatever time.

And the ones who sobbed over and over, I am telling
the truth, never changed their story, he said. End of story.

You've told me this story more than once, more than once telling
me something I never heard before until then, telling

it so well I could almost believe I was there myself,
for all that I was at the time so many miles away.

REVOLUTION

The spinning mills going up in an avalanche of flame.
The vacillating gun turret of the Saracen tank.

The tick and tack of the Remote Bomb Disposal Unit.
The watch you consult to see what has elapsed of the day.

The untrustworthy public clocks, stopped at various times.
The hands sometimes missing or the face pockmarked by shrapnel.

The face-powder compact they discovered in your handbag.
The hands at my spreadeagled body, ankles, hips and groin.

The clicking security cameras watching, watching.
The helicopter trawling the murk with its wand of light.

The public telephone box where I'm trying to get through.
The helicopter hovering on its down-swash of noise.

The way your voice comes over in waves of long-distance call.
The things you tell me of what might become of us for now.

L'AIR DU TEMPS

Nice perfume, I said. Thank you, you said. It was our first date.
I've always wondered about perfumes, I said, what is it?

L'Air du Temps by Nina Ricci, you said, she made it up
just after the War. Spirit of the Times, it was supposed

to evoke the era, the girls in Pompadour hairstyles
blowing kisses everywhere, garlanding the tank turrets.

Lalique designed the flacon later, 1951,
the frosted glass stopper a pair of intertwining doves.

As for the scent, it opens with luminous bergamot
and rosewood, developing a bouquet of gardenia,

violet, jasmine and ylang ylang. Wraiths of green moss
and sandalwood give *L'Air du Temps* its gentle persistence.

The base is powdery orris, cool woods, musk and resins,
permeated with a faint radiant heat of amber.

They say it goes well with pastels and purples, the latter
in every shade from palest lavender to heliotrope.

Fabrics should be near transparent, or crisp and clean, you said.
You were wearing a 1950s blouse of pastel blue.

So what shade would you call that? I said, looking at your blouse.
You looked down at yourself. It's a very, very pale French

blue, you said. It puts me in mind of winters in Paris.
It is frosty, and if you stand in Montmartre you can

see for miles. I'm looking at the patchwork quilt of Paris:
parks, avenues, cemeteries, temples, impasses, arcades.

I can see the house where I was raised, and my mother's house.
I am in her boudoir looking at her in the mirror

as she, pouting, not looking, puts on *L'Air du Temps*, a spurt
of perfume on each wrist before she puts her wristwatch on.

SECOND TAKE

Most of the witnesses we knew then are dead if not gone,
sequestered in havens to become shadows of themselves.

Take Carrick, whose name was a byword for integrity,
bundled into an unmarked car to vanish without trace:

whatever he'd borne witness to must have been worth knowing,
so much so they say he arranged his own disappearance.

Take McCloud, a man notoriously hard of hearing,
whose earpiece was tuned to every whisper in the city:

he fell foul of a so-called cancer of the inner ear,
a steady creep of secrets invading the labyrinth.

Take the others who were given a new identity,
not that we could say for sure who they were in the first place.

Take me, you said, the first time ever you set eyes on me:
for all that I told you then, you took me for what I was.

THE SHADOW

The Glass Bead Game? I said. *Das Glasperlenspiel*, if you like,
you said, not that my German is anything to speak of.

Though I remember, as a verb, *perlen* means to bubble,
as in upwardly streaming pearls of water in a pot

just coming to the boil. As for what went on in the book,
I'm at a loss to say what it was all about, or not.

The game itself was difficult to visualize. I thought
of a chess more infinitely complicated than chess,

played in three dimensions, if not four or five, for the game,
as I understood it, could admit of most anything,

though politics was frowned on. The game was above all that.
A Bach motet, or how the prose style of Julius Caesar

mirrors the cadences of some Early Byzantine hymns,
the calligraphic gestures of a flock of birds at dusk:

these were considered subjects for the Glass Bead Game. Or not.
There were always those who thought the opposite to be true.

The subject of the book becomes a *Magister Ludi*,
Master of the Game. He is skilled in many disciplines.

With a luminous gold stylus he writes a hieroglyph
on the dark, and so initiates a constellation

from which blossom countless others. Were the Game a music
it would require an organ with an infinite number

of manuals, pedals and stops. If geometry, or not,
Pythagoras never dreamed of it. Plato was not close.

Though it originated in the simple abacus,
the wires representing a musical staff and the beads

of various sizes, shapes and colours of glass the notes,
it grew in time to be a model of the universe.

I gather the glass beads became metaphorical beads,
not to be fingered by hand but tuned to some other sense.

At any rate, a Master is not allowed to marry.
Now I remember this one was called Knecht, which means not knight,

but vassal. He is in thrall to the Game. He is assigned
an underling, a Shadow. The Shadow must study him.

It does not do for a Master to have a weak Shadow.
And the Master must be fit to stand up to his Shadow.

Though the Shadow may act in his Master's stead he may not
lay forward proposals of his own. And though he may wear

the Master's robes when occasion demands he can never
be Master himself. Such are the rules of the Glass Bead Game.

So you must cultivate your Shadow, for there is never
one Master but another lies waiting in his shadow,

you said. And what has all of this got to do with Berlin,
I said, and your time there? You don't know how much I missed you.

I kept wondering where you were and what you were thinking.
As did I of you, you don't know the half of it, you said.

Isn't that the trouble? That I don't know the half of it?
Sometimes I wonder if we speak the same language, I said.

You took a sip of cold coffee and stared out the window.
The sun had just come out. Leaf-shadow dappled the cobbles.

It's like this, you said. Those who play the Glass Bead Game don't know
there's a war on they're so wrapped up in themselves and their Game.

You know I was in Berlin for a reason. Yes, I chose
to walk that path, as surely as I chose to go with you.

There's no point in going into what else I might have been.
Then you walked out the door and I followed in your shadow.

THE FETCH

To see one's own doppelgänger is an omen of death.
The doppelgänger casts no reflection in a mirror.

Shelley saw himself swimming towards himself before he drowned.
Lincoln met his fetch at the stage door before he was shot.

It puts me in mind of prisoners interrogated,
of one telling his story so well he could see himself

performing in it, speaking the very words he spoke now,
seeing the face of the accomplice he had invented.

When all is said and done there is nothing more to be said.
No need for handcuffs, or any other restraint. They take

a swab of his sweat from the vinyl chair in which he sat.
Should he ever escape his prison the dogs shall be loosed.

Your death stands always in the background, but don't be afraid.
For he will only come to fetch you when your time has come.

THE STORY OF MADAME CHEVALIER

The swallow flew to my ear from her nest under the eaves.
She told me a stranger was approaching through the forest.

So I climbed to the top of my tall tower and looked out
to see if it was you returning after seven years.

I found you in a clearing. You had changed. But not so much
I didn't know you under the ruin of your cocked hat.

It was evident your memory had been shot to pieces
in the war. You didn't know me from Eve. I took you home.

I bandaged you and bedded you until you got better.
It took you a good nine months not to look at me awry.

Only then did you see the quilt I'd wrapped you in aright.
There are bits of me in here, you said. This must be your work.

I tore up your old shirts the day you enlisted, I said,
and sewed the scraps back together in this crazy pattern.

ZUGZWANG

As the negotiators end by drawing up a form
of words which can be claimed by both sides as a victory;

as on a factory floor in the former East Berlin
the puzzle women puzzle together the shredded files;

as the door handle is sprinkled with fingerprint powder
to trace the guilty hand among so many innocent;

as the old chess master cannot say if ever he learned
the game, since each new game blossoms with new constellations;

as the choreographer charts out moves on a dance floor
like the chalk marks on a snooker table, play having ceased;

as the mad litigant rummages through his suitcase full
of ancient carbon copies to pursue his dubious suit—

so I write these words to find out what will become of you,
whether you and I will be together in the future.

FROM IN BEHIND

the wall
hangings

watched
through slits

is what
is innermost

a voice box
wire grille

crackling on
the darkness

harrowed by
dragon's teeth

a minefield
salted with eyebright

LET US GO THEN

through the trip-
wired minefield

hand in hand
eyes for nothing

but ourselves
alone

undaunted by
the traps & pits

of wasted land
until

you stoop
& pluck

a stem
of eyebright

WATCH

a beam
of intermittent

light flits
across

the window night
after night

touching
your face

through
the helicopter

noise I can
still hear

the tick
of the clock

THE FALLING LEAVES

fall on
the fallen leaves

the rain beats
on the rain

noise beats
on noise

two men shout
& beat

each other
on the street

noise beats on
noise

as you lie
sleeping

STUMBLING

on a tuft
of eyebright

I tore it
from the earth

& found
below

a sightless hoard
of bones

in a coil
of golden hair

a coin
that bore

the head of
a dead king

THE BLIND CONNING TOWER

sits proud
of the dazzle

camouflaged vessel
of which parts

are wrapped
in mirror wrap

the hull so
broken up by

abrupt zigzags
that we deem

the field of vision
to be skewed

her course
impossible to plot

THE DAY BEFORE

yesterday
three crows plucked

my cherry orchard
clean

I shot all three
today

three journeywomen
cloaked in black

came to my door
armed with distaff

scroll & shears
one to spin

one to span
one to snip

IN EACH OTHER'S EYES

we are what
we remember

of each other
more than that

the increments
by which time

gains on us
& then retracts

into a darkness
that we never

knew till now
in whose light

dawning
in whose eyes

BEHIND THE SCREEN

a blip that
should not be

but was as shown
by the scan

the outcome
not yet known

that is to ask
exactly what

it was I saw
a shaft of light

an arrow
driven through

the eye-slit
of a helmet

IN WHOSE EYES

under whose
surveillance

did it look
this way

the road gone
suddenly awry

before giving out
before a wood

beyond which
were no words

for what lay
beyond the ken

of the blind
conning tower

THE STORM WITHOUT

becomes a surf
a vestibule

awash with leaves
the windows creak

from squall to
squall these words

you seethe into
my inner ear

the vestibule
wherein we meet

to founder in
the storm within

to keep at bay
the storm without

FOR HOW LONG

had we waited
months or years

the days & hours
we counted

backwards
to the scan

& forward
to the scan

between the blip
& blip eternity

or time arrested
justified by

what we
do not know

ON LOOKING THROUGH

a speculum
at what

we fear to name
considering

the hereafter
of division

subdivisions
mortally bereft

as all change
must for life

we close our eyes
for fear

of seeing
the immortal cell

UPON SEEING YOU

between two leaves
of a volume

a sprig of eyebright
faded blue

between two doors
along a corridor

of eyebright blue
into an open ward

I walk with flowers
in my hand

to find the one
I'm looking for

between two sheets
you

IT'S THE SAME

old story
but not

as we know
it we thought

it was
a box

until we found
the key on

the verge of
these words

SO IT IS

as when
death draws

nigh death
draws a hush

upon the house
until the one

who is about
to die

cries open
the door

HIS LAST WORDS

were the story is not
over

yet whereof
we cannot

speak until
we hear

the words from
one who has

died
before

whereupon
we begin to

tell what once
was told

LEANING INTO

the picture
of a portal

looming from
the fog

so close we
breathe

on it
the threshold

lost until
we step back

WHATEVER

imponderable
toll time

takes we
cannot tell

the order
of our going

hence until
the next

not even
then

WE SEE

the ways
he smeared into

the grey
with his fingers

rubbing out
what paint

had been
until we see

a child
rubbing fog

from a window
with his sleeve

to reveal more
fog beyond

IN YOUR ABSENCE

wandering from
room to empty

room I do not hear
your silence

in a ward
beyond earshot

time measured
footfall by footfall

drip by drip
until not at all

HOMECOMING

is as yet
indeterminate

depending on
what progress made

on every breath
you draw

bringing you
further on until

little threshold
by threshold

IF EVER

it could be said
to be a box

we found a key
for it but not

as we knew it
the wards

of its lock
turning clockwise

or anti
until something

clicked within
and something gave

an aperture
of daylight

SINGLED BY

the eye and
taken up by

itself it was
shining white

but taken with
sky

a strong hard
blue as before

a remembrance
of other clouds

WHICH CLOUD

I gazed at lying
on my back

on the green grass
of my back yard

billowing full sail
limned with silver

at its edges
before the clouds

of explosion boomed
from the horizon

IN THE PARLOUR

does one look
at who lies there

or take the body
in in glances

no one looking
back the eyelids

motionless
the mouth

sealed as
I look on

him who came
before me

laid out
before me

FIVE FLIGHTS UP

I remember
where I was at

the time but
not the time

whatever yesterday
it was before

descending landing
after landing

I landed in
today

AND

is what
comes before what

comes next
and thus is one

of many antes
and is also going

on and on on
time into forever

and thus is never
before time

BACKTRACKING ON

what one
thinks one said

or what one thinks
or thought one

thought was that
said before

the words
in hindsight

now the story comes
out otherwise

the door you walked
through then long

since closed and all
the truer for that

AS BLADE

to haft before
is meet to after

or as one knife
whets another

as is axe
to helve your life

is honed upon
the sharping stone

of what was nigh
a mortal wound

AS SHARP

is to flat
fast is to slow

as fast is
to feast most

is to least
as high is to low

what lies before
now lies behind if

out of sight
not out of mind

CENTIMETRES

I can do without
let's take it

inch by inch
till inch becomes

a foot a yard
or minutes hours

the months before
the months behind

till inching ever
forward foot by foot

you step over
the threshold of

the future that is
over now

TIME AND

again time
after time to

play in time
as we did with

each other for
the last time

before now that
after without you

I still keep
your time in mind

FROM A WINDOW LEDGE

between your bed
and the view

of the old jail
restlessly

an oscillating fan
sweeps the ward

as a beam might
the yard searching

after what
is long gone

THE EYE

reckons how
many hours

the route from
gutter pipe to

window sill to
overhanging

cornice to
window sill to

parapet to
rooftop ever

after scaling
one's mind

by footholds not
there until

IS ABACUS

to stave as
number is to note

as in a calculus
of pebble dropped

after pebble
drop by drop

into a well
interrupted echoing

after silence
or not

THE TAG

round your wrist
bore a number

your name
and DOB

two weeks after
two stone less

the day you
came home it

slipped off
no need to snip

COMING TO

is not something
you remember

when I ask you
somewhere

the evening after
got lost you must

have been still
high when

I came to see
you hooked up

to the pulse
of drips through

which I heard you
murmur to me

I WONDERED

where you'd
been these past

hours the space
by my side empty

as I turned over
to find you

not there
in my sleep but

elsewhere after
I thought of it

AS ELSEWHERE IS

wherever we
are not there

are as many
elsewheres

as ourselves
remember how

we meet elsewhere
the after-hours

through which
we played

I OPEN THE DOOR

into hall and
over threshold

after threshold
slowly oh

so slowly I bring
you heavy

step by step up
the seventeen

steps of that
flight once trodden

so swiftly as
year over year

to our room
full of light

AS I ROVED OUT

after Arthur Rimbaud, 'Aube'

I embraced the summer dawn. All was still before
the palaces, their waters dead forevermore.

Shade after shadow lingered on the woodland road.
I woke quick, live, warm clouds of breath as on I strode.

Gemstones eyed my passing. Wings arose without sound.
My first adventure happened on a path I found

already littered with pale glints, wherein a flower
spoke her name to me. I blinked. It was no known hour.

I laughed to see the Wasserfall dishevelling itself
in shocks among the pines; climbing shelf by rocky shelf,

I recognized the goddess at the silvered peak.
Voilà! Veil after veil I lifted from her, not to speak

of how my arms were fluttering as I did so.
I did it in the lane. And boldly did I go

across the plain where I betrayed her to the cock.
She fled to the city under the steeple clock,

and beggar-like I tailed her on the marble quays.
Far up the road, beneath a grove of laurel trees,

I wound her in those recollected veils, and realized,
just a little, something of her massive shape and size.

Then dawn and child, finding themselves in the wood,
sank deep down into it. On waking it was noon.

FÉE

after Arthur Rimbaud, 'Fairy'

All for Helen, ornamental oozing saps collogued
in virgin shadows: silent, unmoved, glittering the astral road.

Summer's torrid heat was given over to the mute birds,
inevitable languor to an expensive funeral barge

through winding estuaries of loves long dead;
and perfumes like an evanescent freshet overlaid

the chorus of the Timberwomen to the rumble
of the torrent through the ruined wood, from the cowbells

in the valleys echoing the long cries of the steppes;
all for Helen, bushy furs and shadows quivered, bee-skeps

oozed, the poor shivered, shimmering the celestial legends.
And her eyes, her dancing far superior to a thousand

precious dazzles coldly flowing in, or to the pleasure
of that unique décor, that one and only hour.

SNOW

after Arthur Rimbaud, 'Fleurs'

From a golden staircase—among the silken cords
on gauze of grey, plush velvets lush as greensward,

discs of crystal blackening like bronze when struck
by noon—I see the foxglove open on a ruck

of carpet wrought with silver filigree of eyes
and tresses. Pieces of yellow gold strewn slantwise

over agate, tall piers of pernambuco wood
supporting domes of emerald in the interlude

of bouquets of white satin sporting on ruby sprays,
surround the water-rose's delicate display.

And like a god with huge blue eyes and arms of snow
the sea and sky pull towards the marble terraces

great crowds of white roses rising in crescendo
as forever young forever strong they grow and grow.

ON THE ROAD

after Arthur Rimbaud, 'Enfance'

1

Black-eyed idol, shocked with yellow hair, of no known clan
or ancestry, yet nobler than fable, Mexican

crossed with Flemish; her domain the arrogant azure
and forty shades of greenery which court the shore

called into being by the shipless waves which speak
its placenames of barbaric Slavic, Celtic, Greek.

At the brink of the forest—dream flowers tingle, flash
and flare—the girl with orange lips, her knees sashed

by the glassy flood that gushes from the meadows,
body bare but shimmering and clothed by flora, rainbow,

sea and shadow. Ladies stroll on terraces
adjacent to the sea. There are girls and giantesses,

tall black women proud amid the mossy verdigris,
jewels standing in the fat soil of the seaside groves

and thawing flowerbeds. Young mums the images
of big sisters with their eyes full of pilgrimages;

sultanas, swanky princesses in haughty haute couture
and little foreign girls, and girls in melancholic sweet amour.

Quel ennui, the hours of murmuring, 'Ma chérie,
I know just how you feel . . . He will come round, you'll see.'

2

That's her, the little dead girl, behind the bed of roses.
Mamma, passed away, passes down the steps. To the roses.

Cousin's carriage squeaks on the sand. The sun
sets on little brother (he's in India!) in the red carnation

meadow. And the old men buried, for their part,
bolt upright in the wallflower-covered rampart.

A swarm of golden leaves surrounds the general's house.
You take the red road to the empty inn. We're in the South.

The chateau's up for sale, the shutters hanging loose.
The curate has the keys to the church: it's no longer in use.

Around the park the keepers' cottages lie forlorn,
the fences overgrown with rustling, sky-scraping thorn.

In any case there's nothing to be seen beyond the trees.
The meadows climb to hamlets without anvil or cock.

The sluice gate lies open. O Calvaries
and windmills of the wilderness, the isles of haycock.

3

Magic flowers buzzed. Hill slopes rocked him to and fro.
Fabulously elegant monsters performed a mambo.

Clouds fattening and floating tier upon tier
over the high seas gathered from an eternity of tears.

4

In the woods there is a bird. His song stops you. You blush.
There is a clock that never strikes. You hear the hush.

There is a pothole in which white things seethe around.
There is a lake that goes up, and a steeple that goes down.

There is a little carriage in the copse, abandoned
or it's running away down the road beribboned.

There's a troupe of strolling players and their motley brood
glimpsed on the road through the trees at the edge of the wood.

And then, when you're hungry and thirsty, there's always
somebody to chase you away.

5

I am the saint at prayer on the terrace skyline
like the beasts which graze down to the sea of Palestine.

I am the scholar in the armchair in the dark eyrie.
Rain and branches beat against the casements of the library.

I am the wanderer of the high road through
the blasted dwarfish woods; the roar of sluices

deafens my footsteps. For a long time I sit stunned
by the melancholy gold laundry of the setting sun.

I might well be the child abandoned on the pier
floating out to the high seas, the little muleteer

following the mountain track which climbs to the sky.
The paths are rough, hillocks spiked with gorse nearby.

How still the air! How far away the springs and birds!
This must be the end of the world. Ever onwards upwards.

6
When the bit comes to the bit, let them rent
me this tomb covered in bumpy whitewashed cement,

deep down in the earth. I lean my elbow on
the desk. I read by lamplight, fool enough to con

these boring books again. Enormously remote
above my subterranean salon, houses send down roots,

fogs gather. The muck is red or black. Monstrous
city, endless night! Not so far above, the noxious

sewers. Their walls the very thickness of the globe.
Chasms of azure, walls of fire? I send a probe

into these levels, maybe to discover this is where
moons encounter comets, and pterodactyls whirr.

In hours of bitterness I imagine spheres of sapphire
and of metal. I am master of silence. I hear no choir.

Why then, for all the cynicism that I vaunt,
should the ghost of a vent pale in the corner of my vault?

WHAT GOES ROUND

after Arthur Rimbaud, 'Ornières'

To the right, the summer dawn awakes the leaves,
the mists, the noises of the park, and pales the palings' sheaves.

And the slopes to the left hold in their violet shadows
the thousand quickening ruts of the dewy road.

Fairytale procession! Wagons loaded with animals
of gilded wood, rainbow-hued poles and awnings and panels,

all drawn by twenty galloping dappled circus horses, men
and children bouncing on marvellous animals—twice times ten

vehicles bedecked with flowers, ornate as coaches from a fairy tale,
brimming with children dressed up for a suburban pastoral—

coffins under ebon canopies each swaying their pair
of black plumes to the trot of huge blue and black mares.

SHOELACE TIED

from the French of Jean Follain, 'Soulier renoué'

When evening waves
its bank of clouds
one sees the grass fires
raise their smoke
flowers grow in the sunken lanes
there's still a glimpse of daylight
and a boy in an iron-grey smock
bows to a rut
to tie his shoelace
no slack in his life
no trace of absence.

OUT

Thinking
the end of the world to be
at the horizon the boy walked
for hours; after his people
scoured the fields for miles around
crying his name
to the four winds
to no reply
at twilight they found him
where he'd last been seen
standing in the stable yard
unable to say anything
about where he had been
in that full circle he had walked
beyond 'out'
having no words
for what he had seen
beyond those that were of home.

WITHOUT LANGUAGE

from the French of Jean Follain, 'Sans le langage'

The sadness of voice without language
under a sky of racing clouds
wearies the body
going on endlessly
talking every which where
when noises have made their silences
and substance languishes.
Bunches of keys in their pockets
those that live with death
return home.

IN MEMORY

As he told it
when the boy
he was stumbled
on the well
in the derelict brickyard
deep as a brick mill chimney
leaning over the rim
he shouted
the two syllables
of his name
deep down into it
to hear his echo.
Now that the man
he would become
is dead
that unfathomable
darkness
echoes
still.

THE BURNT ISLAND

from the French of Jean Follain, 'L'île brûlée'

Concerning the burnt island
there is a long memory
of all the shadows of inhabitants
and those of ploughs and harrows.
On a certain morning a great noise
was made and shook all the rooms.
Reality dwells
in a child's hand, writing with such force
on the ruled paper
that by the second line he pierced it through
and made the steel nib bend
then an icy wind arose
which made the naked branches bend.

TIMING DEVICE

As with thunder
the rumble comes
after the flash the shimmer
of a tolled bell stroke
after stroke reverberating
heard one certain day
but now but a glimmer
of all such memories of bells
a newsreel flicker
the skeleton of a building
or its scaffolding
he cannot remember
the number of victims
let alone their names
or in what month of what year
that certain day fell.

THE RAG

from the French of Jean Follain, 'La guenille'

Powerless
to imitate the bird
the rag hangs from the branch
red beside the sweet apple
the bird flown the apple fallen
it stays where it is
flaunting the chill of ages
and its colour in the silence;
men are organizing
in the dark times
not far from this tatter marking
nothing but the space it occupies.

SUNSET

The street lamps come on
one by one
as an armoured car speeds
into the oncoming dark
the north wind picks up
from lamp post
after lamp post
along the stretch of demarcated road
the union
flags begin to flicker in their tatters.

TRAGEDY OF THE TIMES

from the French of Jean Follain, 'Tragique du temps'

However strong the prison door
the wind blows through below
even as in days of yore
a pale sun sometimes flickers on the creases
of an executioner's jerkin.
In a seaside town
music strikes up
and laying aside his hoe
a labourer sits down to contemplate
the amicable bandsmen
destined for massacre
within the year
declaring their belief in the soul eternal
and the resurrected body.

INTERLUDE

He switched on
the radio to silence
followed by applause
and realized
the music was over
now he remembers
in a far-off battle
shells exploding round him
followed by the rumble
of the orchestra of guns that fired them
the speed of sound ago.

OCTOBER THOUGHTS

from the French of Jean Follain, 'Pensées d'octobre'

How good it is
to drink this fine wine
all by oneself
when evening illuminates the coppery hills
no hunter any longer sets his sights
on the lowland game
our friends' sisters
look lovelier than ever
regardless of the threat of war
an insect stops
then starts again.

THROWBACK

Children throwing stones
and bottles over the brick wall
topped with broken bottles
ruby amber green
need not know who
drank the wine
all those years ago
nor what lies on the other side
except that it throws back.

WITHOUT COURAGE

from the French of Jean Follain, 'Sans courage'

New courage is needed
for him who returns home
but there is only time, space
the tail end of a periwinkle blue sky
climbing the stairs
he hears a murmuring repeating
God is dead
man too
he stops, the silence dazzles
he composes a face
to take him on up to the attic rooms
almost empty except for childhood.

TRANSLATION

A boy leans out
the attic window
of an empty house
that overlooks
the countryside he dreams
of flying over by the time
he descends
landing after landing from where
he has been, the house
reoccupies itself
its occupants
addressing him
as if he had not been
changed in the meantime
that is elsewhere.

TRANSFIXION

from the French of Jean Follain, 'Lancinant'

The sleeper's head lolls on to his chest
in the acrid afternoon
of dreams that clutch at his heart.
One hears the footfall on the path
of a man in fine shoes
his youth past
never having worked the land
nor served under armies,
he stops to catch his breath
sets off again counting every step
the smoke of the day blurs.
Of a sudden someone in a village
can no longer read or speak.

TRANSFIGURATION

The valves of one's heart
open and close
to the pulse of blood
without one's knowing it
one can be betrayed.
Feel, says the man laying the boy's fingers
on his wrist,
God never shuts one door
but He opens another.
A great wind blows
in an upstairs room
on whose floor an old man
writhes and speaks in tongues
of the souls that dwell
in the mind
like tongues of fire.

LACED BOOT

from the French of Jean Follain, 'Brodequin'

Methodically tying
a well worn grey lace
under the greening sign
a man has rediscovered
some appreciation
for the relics of old decency
his eyes have seen
these eyelets
ringed with yellow brass
the meandering wrinkles
in a borrowed boot
whose every nail will mark
the humus of the plain
till the day of his death
so many steps away.

ONE DAY WHEN

The boy bows
to do up his lace
the yellow brass
of the monastery bell
shimmers from afar
under a sky blank
as the spaces between
the feint blue lines
of the pages yet to go
in his school notebook.
A red insect trembles
from the green moss
between two flagstones
then begins to creep
towards
the unimaginable horizon.

MANNANÁN MAC LIR
SANG THESE VERSES

Bran thinks it marvellous to sail
    his coracle over a clear sea
while for me my swift chariot
    drives over a flowery plain

Bran cleaves the clear sea
    with the prow of his keen boat
while for me the Plain of Delights
    heaves with a thousand flowers

over a clear sea Bran beholds
    wave after rolling wave
while on the Plain of Feats I see
    a host of crimson-headed flowers

while the seahorses' white manes
    are combed by Bran's roving eye
flowers pour forth streams of honey
    in Manannán mac Lir's domain

the glassy sea where you are found
    the shining ocean that you sail
is blossoming with green and yellow
    truly it is solid ground

those speckled salmon leaping
    from the womb of the white sea
truly they are calves and lambs
    sporting without enmity

though you see but one charioteer
            on the many-flowered plain
you do not see the many steeds
            abroad on its broad bosom

a huge army shimmers on the plain
            brimming with every colour
banners of silver and cloths of gold
            in jubilant array

shaded by the spreading trees
            men and women freely play
a game of such delight and ease
            they know no sin nor wrong

along the top of a waving wood
            has your coracle sailed
under the keel of your little boat
            are trees laden with fruit

a wood of blossom and bud
            bearing the scent of the true vine
an imperishable wood
            glorious with leaves of gold . . .

therefore let Bran row steadily on
            it is not far to the Land of Women
and before sunset he shall reach Emain
            and its manifold pleasures

[from *Immram Brain* (*The Voyage
of Bran*), 8th century Irish]

Int én bec	*The little bird*
ro léc feit	*that whistled shrill*
do rinn guip	*from the nib of*
glanbuidi	*its yellow bill:*
fo-ceird faíd	*a note let go*
ós Loch Laíg,	*o'er Belfast Lough—*
lon do chraíb	*a blackbird from*
charnbuidi	*a yellow whin*

[from the 9th century Irish]

NOTES

XIII   'Aistrigh liom siar sa ród…': See Pádraigín Ní Uallacháin's translation of 'Úirchill a' Chreagáin' in *A Hidden Ulster: People, Songs and Traditions of Oriel*, (Four Courts Press, 2003). Also https://www.orielarts.com/songs/uirchill-a-chreagain

1   *Colm Cille recited*: The language of the poem is eleventh or twelfth century. Colm Cille (literally, church dove) died in AD 597. A slightly different version was published in Stuart McWilliams, ed., *Saints and Scholars* (essays in honour of Hugh Magennis, DS Brewer, 2012).

42   'Switch': A kind of *aisling*. See note on 'The Display Case' below. Among the definitions of *malairt*, according to Dinneen's Irish-English Dictionary, are: 'a change, alteration (as in a text), exchange, swop, barter, dealing, traffic, recompense; difference, variety, opposite; act of changing (as in one's religion, etc.), altering, alternating, etc.; m. *éadaigh*, a change of clothes …'

57   *Opera Et Cetera*: The 1998 publication is in four sections: *Letters from the Alphabet*; *Et Cetera*, poems named after Latin tags; *Alibi*, versions of poems from the Romanian of Stefan Augustin Doinas; and *Opera*, poems taking their names from the NATO phonetic alphabet, officially denoted as the International Radiotelephony Spelling Alphabet.

65   *Jacta Est Alea*: The die is cast (quoted as said by Caesar at the crossing of the Rubicon).

66   *Graecum Est: Non Legitur*: This is Greek: it is not read (placed against a Greek word in medieval MSS, a permission to skip the hard words).

73   *The Alexandrine Plan*: Facing French texts are included in the 1998 publication.

80   'The Blue Shamrock': A kind of *aisling*. See below.

83   '1798': A kind of *aisling*. See below.

91   'The Display Case': 'Creggan churchyard' refers to the celebrated *aisling* 'Úirchill a' Chreagáin', written by Art Mac Cumhaigh of Creggan in South Armagh. The *aisling* is a type of allegorical poem which reached its height in the eighteenth century when the Irish language was beginning to decline. Typically, a beautiful woman (*spéirbhean*, or 'sky-woman') appears to the poet in a dream and exhorts him to redress Ireland's troubles. *Aisling* is usually translated as 'dream vision', and it is understood to be such in Irish. It belongs to a European genre which includes Dante's *Divina Commedia*. I like to think *aisling* comes from *ais*, meaning 'back', as in the expression *ar ais arís*, 'back again', and *ling*, 'to leap or spring'. Thus, *aisling* could mean a backward leap, as the poet wants his country back, lamenting the disappearance of the old Gaelic order and its lordly patronage of poets, sometimes upbraiding those who are turning to English. Some people like to think that the *aisling* was one of the inspirations for the United Irishmen rebellion of 1798. And when I think of *aisling*, I think of *aistriú*, which can mean a revolution, a spin on its generic meanings of change or exchange, or of journeying, or of moving things from one place to another, i.e. translation. '*Aistrigh liom siar sa ród go tír dheas na meala*,' says the *spéirbhean* to the poet in Creggan churchyard, 'Journey back (or west) with me along the road to the sweet land of honey … in whose halls you will delight, being enticed by strains of song.' The aisling (I drop the italics, since it has entered the Oxford English Dictionary) can be thought of as a metaphor for musical and poetic inspiration.

93   *Breaking News*: 'Gallipoli', 'War', and 'Sedan' have been 'translated' from William Howard Russell's reports of the Crimean War (1853–56) and the Franco-Prussian War (1870–71).

105   *For All We Know*: The 2008 publication consisted of Part One and Part Two, each with thirty-five poems with identical titles in the same sequence.

152   *In The Light Of*: The 2012 publication consists of verse translations of prose poems from Arthur Rimbaud's *Illuminations*.

160   *From Elsewhere*: The 2014 publication consists of translations from the French poet Jean Follain, faced by 'original' poems inspired by those translations: spins or takes on them as it were. Translations of the translations in other words.